The
Force
Within Us

How our human instincts
motivate everything we do

by Paul Bergen Abbott

Published by The Abbott Company
Crawfordsville, Indiana, USA

ISBN 978-0-9885870-0-7

This book is dedicated to my mother and father, my grandparents and all my ancestors who survived and reproduced and passed on to me the instincts that motivated me to write this book.

Contents

Who speaks to the instincts speaks to the deepest in mankind, and finds the readiest response.

—Amos Bronson Alcott

Chapter 1
The Incident

It was a pleasant summer day at the Brookfield Zoo. Visitors of all ages were gathering around the animal exhibits, unaware of the frightening incident that was about to happen.

At the gorilla exhibit, people had an excellent view of the animals. The spectators were safe, standing on an 18-foot-high walkway surrounded by a four-foot-high fence. They needed that separation because a gorilla can be a dangerous animal. It has enormous strength compared to humans and large, sharp teeth. An aggressive gorilla could easily injure or kill any of the visitors, if only that fence and 18 feet of separation weren't there.

To protect the keepers, who sometimes had to enter the gorilla enclosure, three high-pressure hoses had been installed. If needed, keepers could aim blasts from those hoses at the gorillas' feet to hold them back.

As a mother and a three-year-old boy approached the gorilla enclosure, the boy ran ahead, excited to see the great apes. Temporarily distracted, the mother didn't notice the boy climbing the fence to get a better view of the big animals.

Then the visitors gasped. The boy, teetering on the fence, lost his balance and fell—careening 18 feet to the concrete floor below— right in the midst of those powerful gorillas!

The boy was not moving. He was unconscious from the fall and bleeding from his injuries. He lay there motionless, at the mercy of those great beasts. Seeing this, visitors held their breath.

What happened next would have been hard to believe, were it not for a video that was shot by one of the visitors. It showed one of the gorillas, a 150-pound female, moving toward the small boy. What would this powerful animal—who had never been face-to-face with a young human before—do to the injured boy?

As everyone watched, the massive gorilla bent down over the unconscious boy, gently picking him up in her powerful arms and carrying him to a door that was used by the keepers. The animal laid the boy down and stepped back, giving the keepers space to enter and remove the boy.

The boy was safe. The gorilla was hailed as a hero. The incident was front-page news in papers in Chicago and other cities across the country. "Gorilla Saves Tot in Brookfield Zoo Ape Pit" said the *Chicago Tribune*. It was a sensation.

How would you explain this gorilla's behavior? Ask anyone, and you're likely to hear something like, "It was instinct. The female ape was following its mothering instinct to protect a youngster. She probably felt the need to take care of this young creature that was obviously hurt. She wanted to take it to a creature of its own kind who might be able to help it."

While you and I weren't there to see it, we can easily imagine the scene. On one side of that concrete barrier were the humans. On the other side were the gorillas. Both groups were watching the same scene. Both groups were feeling the same anguish, the same concern for the young boy who was lying injured and bleeding between them.

We can imagine both groups sensing the same protective instinct, wanting to somehow help the injured youngster, wanting to somehow scoop him up and take him to a safe place.

On one side, one individual moved. She stepped forward and carried the youth to safety. It could have been one of the people if that person could have reached the boy. But it was one of the gorillas who took the action.

In this situation the animal's instincts were clear to see, as they often are in animals. On that day at the zoo, the people there must have felt the pull of the same instinct, a feeling deep within us telling them that we must protect our young. It's a force that could have moved any individual there, human or gorilla, to take action.

We readily understand that animals are driven by instincts. There's little to hide instincts in animals. A dog will fetch, a cat will chase a string, a salmon will swim upstream. You can plainly see the animals' instincts in action, motivating their behavior.

But it's not so easy to see instincts in humans. We hide them, burying them under lessons we have learned. "Don't pinch your little brother," we may hear at an early age. "Get good grades in school," we may hear later. "Be nice to your boss," is another lesson that we may learn.

We learn to conceal our delight in tormenting our siblings, and we may avoid bothering our little brother. We suppress our desire to go out and play, and as a result, we may stay inside and study our lessons. We hide our negative feelings toward the people who control our lives, so our demanding boss may never know when we are offended. We cover up our instincts. We hide them.

That's why we humans are such mysterious creatures. We're very difficult to understand. "Why did he do that?" we wonder. "What makes her tick?" we ask.

If we could only see the instincts at work inside us, we should be better able to uncover our mystery. If we could uncover our human instincts, we could better understand our human nature.

That's what we're about to do. We are about to uncover the force within us.

We are just an advanced breed of monkeys
on a minor planet of a very average star.

Stephen Hawking

Chapter 2
What are Our Instincts?

For centuries, philosophers, physicians and other serious thinkers have tried to understand human nature. Shakespeare expressed his view of human nature through his writings. Freud wrote volumes about human nature. These thinkers described human nature in various ways, but they all determined that there are some aspects of human behavior that are universal, present in all people everywhere. For example, Plato said, " All men are by nature equal, made all of the same earth by one Workman."

Whether people are living in large metropolitan cities or in small primitive tribes, people do many things that are the same. Consider a smile: In any culture around the world a smile is recognized as a friendly sign. Consider the response to a gift: Everywhere on earth, people react to a gift with a thankful response. And consider how we treat our kids: Parents everywhere protect their children. These are universal human behaviors. They're the same in any country and any culture, primitive or advanced. They're the same among all people. Obviously, something in us has to be driving our consistent behaviors, our basic human nature. It's our human instincts.

What are our instincts?

Instincts are the force within us that makes us what we are. We feel them in our every thought. We see them in our every action. They guide us and define us. Sometimes they compel us strongly. Sometimes they merely whisper softly within us. They're always active, always wanting. They're with us from our first breath to our last.

Instincts are our true nature, our true self, the core of our being. Without them we would not move. With them, we can accomplish wonders. They are neither good nor bad until we express them. They are the starting point of our selves. They are we.

Yes, we humans do have instincts. And they are very important. Our instincts give us the incentive to do things. They are the force that makes us want to act in certain ways.

When you root for the home team, that's motivated by an instinct. When you feel love for your child, that's motivated by an instinct. When you feel anger at a villain in a movie, that's motivated by an instinct. In fact, when we humans do anything, we are motivated by instincts. Beneath everything we do, our instincts are at work.

Instincts motivate our behavior. That, in fact, is a good definition of an instinct:

> An instinct is a genetically-based motivation.

How important are our instincts?

Instincts are a key if you want to understand us humans. They sit quietly inside of us, making us feel, "I want this." They work by giving us feelings. They don't work by rational thoughts or by logic. The feeling of love a mother has when she looks at her young baby is an instinct at work. The feeling of rage a parent feels if he sees his child being bullied is an instinct at work. The feeling of fear an auto driver has if she sees a car bearing down on a collision course is an instinct at work.

We usually label the feelings our instincts produce with the name *emotions*. Emotions are the tools that our instincts use to motivate us. These emotions can be strong—like fear, anger or jealousy. Or they can be more subtle—like the desire for recognition or the want for freedom.

Sometimes the emotions produced by our instincts are clearly visible, as when an angry athlete yells at a referee after a questionable call. Sometimes instinctive emotions are quite subtle, as when a young girl primps for a prom date. Sometimes they are hidden, like when an insulted performer conceals his anger at a heckler.

The feelings produced by our instincts motivate and guide us from our birth and throughout our life, at every moment, in every action, and in every situation. They establish what we care about. They tell us what is important. And they can make us feel fear and concern when we see a young boy fall into a gorilla enclosure.

Where did our instincts come from?

Our instincts came from our ancestors. Every one of our ancestors, going back as far as anyone can trace, passed on to us his and her nature. And each of our ancestors had the same basic instincts. That's because, if you trace far enough back into our ancestors' past, all of us have descended from the same few individuals.

That makes our individual instincts all very much the same, except for random variations that have come into us since our ancestors got together, however long ago that was. Whatever characteristics our ancestors had, we have. All of us are born with these characteristics.

Can we change our instincts?

The best answer to that question is no, we can't change our instincts. They're built into us under the direction of our DNA.

There are, however, some unusual conditions that can change our instincts. Our instincts can change over a lifetime as our bodies and brains mature and age. They can change as the result of damage to our brain such as an accident or disease. They could change as a result of brain surgery or the use of drugs. But, generally speaking, we're stuck with our instincts just as they are, and that's not a bad thing.

It's not bad because we have an infinite way to control the effects of our instinct: our culture. We can, and do, use our culture to satisfy the motivations our instincts give us. When we feel the force of our instincts motivating us, we can decide what we will do about it. And anything we decide to do is part of our culture. There's no limit to what we can accomplish with our culture. Through our culture we have already figured out how to fly even higher and faster than birds, talk to people on the other side of the world, go to the moon, and make a really good apple pie. We'll talk more about our culture.

Aren't animals the only creatures with instincts?

We're not surprised to see instinctive behavior in animals. Without being taught, birds fly, dogs bark, lions hunt and gorillas groom each other. That's all instinctive behavior.

It's not much of a stretch to see that we humans are instinctive, too. Think about it: Birds, dogs, lions and gorillas are all mammals. We humans are also classified as mammals. And if you compare a human brain to the brain of other mammals, you'll see a strong resemblance. The same parts of the brain are there, including the parts that are thought to be the basis of our instincts. That's why it's not surprising that, when the boy fell into the gorilla pit at the zoo, the gorilla and the people had similar instinctive reactions.

Even though we humans have further-developed brains that support our special intelligence, we still have the same basic brain parts that support instincts in other mammals. And, like that gorilla at the zoo, we naturally feel a protective instinct when we see a young individual in distress. We naturally are motivated by our instincts.

Does having instincts like other animals mean we humans are not intelligent? Of course not! We have highly developed brains. We can invent vehicles to move us at superhuman speeds. We can learn other languages and communicate with people on the other side of the world. We can even send people to the moon. We're very smart creatures, we humans. We can figure out how to do amazing things, but we're always motivated by our instincts. Our instincts set us moving; then our intelligence guides our accomplishments. You'll read more about this in the next chapter.

Chapter 3
Where are Our Instincts?

Our instincts exist in the place that's the center of our world: our brain. Everything we know, think and feel is right there inside the top of our head, concentrated in a grapefruit-sized glob of gelatinous stuff. It's not impressive to look at, our brain, but it holds our very essence. In our brain is our awareness, our intelligence, our thoughts and our feelings. It's not just *some* of what we know—It's *all* of it.

People didn't understand the importance of our brains until recently. For centuries our ancestors couldn't figure out what was the purpose of that strange stuff in our heads. The ancient Egyptians thought the brain was totally unimportant. When they prepared mummies for their journeys into the afterlife, the Egyptians carefully removed all the internal organs and placed them in the tomb with the well-wrapped body—but they removed the brain and threw it away!

For a long time, it was a widely-accepted idea that the center of our thoughts and feelings was our heart, not our brain. It seemed very reasonable; the heart is always active, constantly beating while our thoughts and feelings are active. When the heart stops, the thoughts and feelings stop. This seemed like an obvious conclusion. It was so obvious that the idea of the heart as the center of our being persisted for many centuries.

Today, science has conclusively shown that the heart has one job: to pump blood. It does not host any of our thoughts and feelings; that's the job of our brain.

But even though now we know better, we continue to follow the romantic notion that the heart is the center of our world. We talk about our "heartfelt" feelings. "We sing "My heart cries for you" and "If I give my heart to you" and "Heart of my heart."

It's handy to think about the heart as our center. It's customary. It's romantic. It seems rather beautiful. And, no doubt, we'll continue to invoke our heart at weddings, in greeting cards and on Valentine's Day. We'll keep putting it on our bumper stickers to declare "I ♥ NY" and "I ♥ My Dog." We English speakers will go on calling our dear ones "sweetheart." Spanish speakers will whisper "corazón" (heart) to their loved ones. French speakers will pine for "mon cœr" (my heart).

There's another wrong idea about the location of our emotions, and it's a bit less romantic. For a long time, many people thought that the center of our emotions was in our intestinal tract—our gut. That idea goes back many centuries, at least as far as the ancient Greeks and Hebrews. Today we still sometimes refer to "gut feelings" or "gutting it out." And, of course, we sometimes get digestive problems due to emotional upsets or stress. Our intestinal tract is equipped with millions of nerve cells, and there are so many that it's sometimes referred to as our "second brain." But it's not a brain. It doesn't think. It doesn't harbor any of our instincts.

The real center of our being is our brain, not our heart or our gut. We now know that. The brain has been called "the three-pound universe," since it contains everything we know and feel. No matter how vast, complicated or mysterious our universe is, all we know, all that we feel and all of our awareness is right there in that most amazing of all our organs, our brain.

How is the brain involved with instincts?

Instincts, like everything else we think and feel, take effect in our brain. Instincts exist in our brain as patterns of activity. The brain is genetically equipped to do many instinctive things. These basic instincts are there naturally, creating motivations, mental conditions that drive us to do things.

To understand how instincts work in the brain, let's use, as an example, one of the most prominent instincts, the instinct to find a mate.

A lot of scientific research has been aimed at understanding how our brain works in seeking a mate. One of the researchers, Helen Fisher, has documented how certain electrical and chemical activity operates within the brain to create feelings that motivate us. She has reported many of her findings in her books *Why We Love* and *Anatomy of Love*.

According to Dr. Fisher, one of the important brain chemicals is *oxytocin*. Ah, yes, oxytocin, how we dearly love thee! We would climb the highest mountain, swim the deepest ocean, do anything to feel your heavenly presence in our brain!

10

Oxytocin is wonderful. It's the magic potion that tells us we're experiencing pleasure. It appears in the brain when it's stimulated by certain experiences, telling us, "This is joy, beauty and happiness. This is love." Oxytocin is sometimes called the "love hormone."

Oxytocin is generated in our brain when we see the face of a beautiful baby, a cute puppy or some individual that we have accepted as a loved one. It's generated during an orgasm, producing a pleasurable bonding urge directed toward the partner. And oxytocin is released in great amounts during childbirth, creating the euphoric feeling that mothers often describe as a strong loving and bonding urge directed toward their newly-released offspring. It's also generated when breast feeding.

Do mothers have an instinct to love their babies? You bet they do! And what we describe as an instinct is aided and abetted by a chemical called oxytocin, along with other chemicals and other stimuli. That's how our instincts work.

Babies have characteristics that have been shown to generate oxytocin in us. Babies have large heads, big, prominent eyes, quaint baby voices, light-colored hair, soft skin and small size. These are features that tend to produce oxytocin when we see them. We often describe the experience positively, blurting out, "How cute!" or "How precious!"

When we encounter these baby-like characteristics in other places, they often produce a similar instinctive reaction. Consider the baby-like voice of singer Brenda Lee. Many people instinctively like it. Consider characteristics that are appreciated in beautiful women: large prominent eyes, soft skin, light-colored complexion and hair. Men like this. And they like the oxytocin these characteristics generate.

And don't we love baby animals! We coo over puppies, kittens, little calves and baby deer. In animated films we instinctively like characters with baby-like characteristics. Think about the Disney characters Mickey Mouse, Porky Pig and Elmer Fudd—big head and eyes, rather like young children. And consider more recent cute characters like Boo, the adorable little girl in the movie "Monsters, Inc." Or Russell, the wide-eyed Wilderness Explorer in the movie "Up." Another example: the big-eyed kids in paintings by Margaret Keane that have been widely popular, instinctively liked.

Oxytocin is a key factor in our loving instincts. It bonds us to our mates. It urges us to protect our children. It's present in animals that experience similar instincts. It has even been found in elephants when they see an elephant baby. It's obviously at work when you see zoo visitors exclaiming about the cute baby animals. We all have instincts, even the animals. And the messengers of these instincts are brain chemicals like oxytocin, vasopressin, dopamine, norepinephrine, serotonin and others.

What are instincts like?

You can't see, touch, smell or taste instincts. They aren't physical things, though they have a physical basis: our DNA. Inside every cell in our bodies are teensy little strands of protein that have an almost unpronounceable name, *Deoxyribonucleic acid*. To make it simple, we just call it DNA. These are the "building blocks" that specify that we are human beings, not apes, not trees, not cabbages. And DNA specifies what are our instincts.

We are fond of saying that something is "in your blood" if it's an inherited characteristic. We talk about royal bloodlines and blood relatives. That's because people used to believe that our blood holds the prescription that makes each of us who we are. Of course, science has shown that's not how it works. And even though we still use the phrase "in your blood" to describe inherited characteristics, we now know it's really a matter of DNA, which is in every cell of our bodies.

Our DNA stores information. It stores that information the way a computer does, in digital form. Here's how a digital computer works: Inside a computer, some very, very complex information is stored in groups of two digits: 1's and 0's. If you put a lot of 1's and 0's together, you can have something like this: 01101001—or 10110101. That first bunch of 1's and 0's could mean one thing, while the second bunch could mean something completely different. Switch any one of those 0's to a 1—or vice versa—and you've changed the meaning of those digits.

Inside our bodies, our DNA stores information in a similar digital way. But instead of having two digits, like 1's and 0's, our DNA has four digits called A's, G's, C's and T's*. Each of these letters represents a little glob of protein called a *nucleotide*. When these little globs are strung together, they form a code that's the blueprint for a human being. Our bodies are built according to this four-digit code.

There are quite a lot of these little globs of protein—three billion in each and every cell of a human—which means that some very complex results can be stored this way. It's all in our DNA code in this four-digit format, including the shape of our hands, the color of our eyes, the texture of our hair and the shape of our nose. Our DNA code also specifies how our brains are built and how they operate.

What else does DNA specify? Our instincts! And since our DNA is more than 99 percent identical in all humans, that's good evidence that we must all share the same basic human instincts.

Can we see our instincts?

It's easy to see instincts in action in young mammals, like dogs and cats. Soon after they are born, puppies and kittens instinctively suck milk from their mothers. The baby animals cry, making noises to indicate they need something. They physically move to be near others of their own kind, like their litter mates and their mothers.

At an early stage of development, human babies do the same instinctive things: sucking milk from their mothers or from bottles, crying when they need something, seeking the comfort of contact with their mothers. Human babies don't have to be taught to do any of these things. This is instinctive behavior, genetically-driven.

Later, human babies continue to develop. They start with a liquid diet and eventually, when more solid food is placed in their mouths, they instinctively chew and swallow it. Without being taught, they begin to crawl, moving their arms and legs in motions that are instinctive. They start to vocalize cute sounds that their parents like to pretend are words. Later these sounds actually become words, as the instinct to talk motivates the babies to imitate sounds they hear. Their crawling motions become more organized, and they eventually stand up (often with help from excited parents) and they begin to walk, following a uniquely human instinct to move around on two feet.

---

*In case you wondered, A, G, C and T are abbreviations. The full names for these nucleotides are adenine (A), guanine (G), cytosine (C), and thymine (T). A group of these is called a gene, a group of genes is called a chromosome. This four-digit genetic code is found in all living things, including all plants and animals.

13

Later, we no longer see purely instinctive human behavior. The babies' sounds become real words, and the baby learns the language of the people around them. The baby learns that certain behaviors draw praise from its parents. It learns that if it asks in certain ways, its parents will give it pretty toys. As it grows, it learns to prefer certain people who will give it ice cream and birthday presents and, later, lend it the car. The child acquires *culture*.

How can you recognize an instinct?

Look for *feelings*. Look for emotion. Emotions are the tool of our instincts. Instincts motivate us through feelings. When you feel joy, pleasure, sadness, envy, love, hate or other emotions, you're feeling your instincts at work.

While instincts are our primary motivators, our feelings almost always involve some amount of culture. Perhaps you may see the good fortune of another person and you feel envy—that's culture. Perhaps you were severely hurt by another person and you feel hate—that's more culture. Culture consists of your experience and your learning, and it can strongly affect your feelings. But the feelings themselves come from your instincts.

Another way to recognize an instinct at work is if you feel *love*. Love is a feeling. When you love something, you're dealing with an instinct. Instincts motivate you toward the things you love. Of course, that feeling of love is usually also based on some piece of culture, something you've learned. Maybe you've learned that the person you love has qualities that you admire. That's culture. But those qualities have triggered the flow of oxytocin or other pleasure chemicals in your brain. That's instinct.

Let's scale down that feeling of love and say that you *like* something. Is that an instinct at work? Yes. That liking is a feeling, and feelings come from our instincts.

For example, let's say you like french fries. To have that liking, first you must have an instinct to feed yourself, to satisfy your hunger. There's the instinct in action. And because of that instinct, at some time in your life you've looked for food, found french fries and sampled them. And you've learned to eat them in preference to other foods you might eat.

14

So you like french fries. 1) What's the instinct? To feed yourself. 2) What's the culture? You've learned that french fries are an acceptable way to satisfy that instinct.

Feelings are a sure indicator of instincts at work. Strong or weak, our emotional feelings all come from our instincts. Our culture can direct and modify these feelings, but culture can't create feelings. That's the job of our instincts.

Men ought to know that from nothing else but the brain come joys, delights, laughter and sports, and sorrows, griefs, despondency, and lamentations.

—Hippocrates

Chapter 4
We've Got Culture!

All this talk about instincts motivating our behavior may sound demeaning. After all, aren't we more than mere animals, blankly responding to primitive urges, completely unable to make rational decisions?

Good question. Good because it brings up the other thing that determines our behavior: our *culture*. Culture is the rational part of the picture.

When an instinct gives us an emotional urge, we use culture to decide what to do about it. If our instinct says, "I really feel angry!" Culture may say, "I must not strike out. This is not the time or place. I'll just count to ten and think about it."

Culture is our claim to fame as humans. Since the most ancient times, we humans have been figuring out how to do things. That's how we've created our culture. We dramatically exceed all other creatures in the things we've developed and the things we know. Our brains have an impressive cerebral cortex, bigger and better than all other creatures in relation to our body size. Like other creatures, we're motivated by our instincts. But unlike other creatures, we use our sophisticated brains to figure out how to get what we want.

Culture consists of everything we've learned. It's everything that each of us knows and all that our entire human history has developed. It's our knowledge about all the people around us. It's what our society puts into our customs and our laws. It's the good stuff and the bad, the myths and the facts, the old ways and the new fads.

Culture is our *physical* tools, like books and shoes and automobiles. It's our *technology* tools like teamwork, education and manufacturing. It's our *knowledge* tools like books and science and language. Everything we know, everything we use, everything we have—that's our culture.

Human nature is a balance between instinct and culture, with the *instinct* providing the motivation and the *culture* guiding the action. This *instinct/culture* combination has sometimes been described as *nature/nurture* or *genetics/learning*. They all mean the same thing. Here we'll call it *instinct/culture*.

How do instincts and culture work together?

There's a clear difference between our instincts and our culture. Here's a comparison:

Instinct	Culture
Comes from DNA	Comes from learning
Born with it	Acquired
Generally powerful	Power varies from strong to weak
Unchangeable	Changeable
Emotional	Rational
From the primitive part of the brain we share with animals	From the more modern part of our human brain
Gives us goals	Gives us tools
Consists of feelings	Consists of thinking
Motivates us	Directs us in satisfying our instincts

This list describes instinct and culture in their pure forms. Looking at it this way, we can see a clear distinction between the two. But when you look for instinct and culture in human behavior, it's usually very difficult to know which is which. Human behavior is a bewildering mix of these two factors. When we watch the behavior of any human more than a few hours old, we are seeing the combined effects of both instinct and culture.

Among living creatures, we humans are kings of culture. This is in contrast to animals around us. They act mainly according to their instincts. Following their instincts, dogs bark and put their noses down to follow scents—without ever having attended a canine academy. Lions stalk prey and attack their sources of food—without ever having read *Hunting* magazine. Birds leap from their nests to take off and fly—without any pilot's licenses. It's all instinctive.

True, some birds appear to learn some of their songs from other birds, individual lions learn specialized roles in their hunting activities with their companions, and dogs can learn their guardian's commands to "sit" and "stay"—though they often have trouble overcoming their instinct to bark when given the command, "no bark." All of these animal species show evidence of learning some culture, but their instincts still dominate their activity.

Culture is a much bigger influence in people than in animals. To see this, let's step back and take a look at our culture. It's a complex mixture of things we've found and things we've developed. To see how this works, let's take a simple example, the instinct to feed ourselves:

To satisfy this instinct, we've developed a culture that's extremely complex: We've learned to put seeds in the ground and harvest the plants that grow. Then we use parts of those plants to make a salad or bread or pizza.

That's just the start of our food culture. We've also developed massive industries to produce and distribute our food. And we've invented devices to prepare and consume our food: ovens and pots and pans and food processors, plates and forks and chopsticks and bowls. When we sit down to a meal, we're motivated by a simple, pure instinct—to feed ourselves—but we're satisfying it by applying our very complex culture.

Our instincts motivate us to feed ourselves. Our culture satisfies that instinct. It's a simple combination. This instinct/culture teamwork happens inside of us every day, every hour, every minute. It's how we humans operate.

Our culture for feeding ourselves is indeed quite complex. But like the complexity of our culture, our instincts are also complex. They are not limited to the one pure instinct we just looked at, the instinct to feed ourselves. Let's look further at other instincts that are involved.

When we feed ourselves, powerful *social instincts* also influence how and what we eat. We famously like to eat in the company of other people (and famously feel uncomfortable dining alone in a restaurant). This is an expression of our social instincts. We like to be with others of our own kind. We eat certain foods that connect us with our national and ethnic heritage: Hungarian goulash, American hamburgers and fries, Chinese noodles, Korean kim chi, Irish shepherd's pie. These are expressions of our instinct to affiliate with others whom we identify as our family and friends. As an example of another instinct at work, we may dine in a romantic setting, expressing our instinct to seek a mate. These other instincts are often mixed with the instinct to feed ourselves.

Can we separate instincts and culture?

Watch people doing things. Try to separate the effect of instincts from the effect of culture. It's very, very difficult, if not impossible. For example, imagine a young woman running to catch a bus. It's a simple action. What instincts could be involved?

Maybe there's the instinct *to feed oneself*—she may be late for supper if she misses the bus. Maybe there's the instinct for *companionship*—she may be joining friends. Maybe there's the instinct for *self esteem*—she may not want to be embarrassed to have to admit she didn't get to the bus stop in time. We could go on and on speculating about what instincts are involved in this single piece of behavior—running to catch a bus. Obviously, there are lots of instincts.

But wait—there's also the matter of culture. This same behavior involves oodles of culture. First, there's the *bus*, a very useful invention of our culture. The bus runs on a *schedule*, and a schedule is one more neat gift of our modern culture that allows us and the bus to be in the same place at the same time. And if the bus driver sees the lady running, he may indulge in a pleasant *social courtesy* of holding the door open—another very nice piece of culture.

Imagine how useful it would be if we could analyze and separate our instincts and our culture. We would have a far greater understanding of ourselves. We would be better able to resolve human problems and increase the quality and harmony of our lives.

That, in a neat package, is the point of this book: To recognize the importance of instincts in our lives, and to see how they motivate us and mix with our culture.

If we understand our instincts and culture better, we may not be such mysterious creatures. We may not have to keep asking ourselves questions like, "What makes him act that way?" or "What does she really want?" or "How can I help them understand each other?" We may have better answers to questions like this.

We need to examine further both instincts and culture. We can also find out how scientists can determine: What part of our behavior is instinct? and What part is culture? That's the fun thing we'll do soon. It's a fascinating cruise through a world of joy, pride, anger, altruism, sex—and other enthralling topics!

You put too much stock in human intelligence,
it doesn't annihilate human nature.

—Philip Roth, American Pastoral

Chapter 5
Beauty is in the Eye of the Beholder

A good place to start in understanding how our instincts work is with the old saying, "Beauty is in the eye of the beholder." This has been said so many times, and for so long, that no one knows for certain where it began. These exact words appear in a novel, *Molly Bawn*, written by Margaret Wolfe Hungerford way back in 1868. And long before that—about 300 years before that, to be exact—William Shakespeare said the same thing in his much more elaborate phraseology.

This beauty saying is old because many people understand its basic truth: that we perceive things according to the way we look at them. What seems like beauty to one person may not seem like beauty to another person. It's not the shape of a face that's beautiful; it's the way a person is equipped to see that face.

Does a dog kept by a beauty queen love its keeper more than a dog kept by a grizzly old hermit? Look at dogs and their keepers and you'll probably decide that dogs can love their keepers regardless of how pretty they are—pretty by human standards, that is. It seems that dogs don't see beauty the way humans do. Why not? Because of their instincts. Dogs obviously don't have instincts that value a human's appearance the way humans do. A face that humans would consider to be pretty seems to be no more interesting to a dog than a face that humans would consider to be ugly.

That example makes the point that a face is a face, and whether or not it's pretty depends on the instincts of who or what is observing it. Beauty is not in the face. It's in the eye of the beholder.

That's the way our instincts work. They give values to the things around us. We may think one thing is pretty. We may think another thing is scary. We may think one thing is desirable. We may think another thing is repulsive. Those qualities are not in those things, they are in us, the beholders. Our instincts are constantly at work, making things seem to have certain qualities.

If the dog example seems a bit remote, let's take an example closer to home. Let's introduce a five-year-old boy. We'll call him Johnny. He's typical for his age, completely average. And let's ask young Johnny about girls.

"Yuk!" says five-year-old Johnny. "I don't care about girls. I don't even like them very much."

To Johnny, girls aren't anything special. And if you ask him, "Are girls pretty?" he'll probably say that he doesn't think so. Being pretty isn't even something he thinks about when he's around girls. In his eyes, he doesn't see much real beauty in them.

In fact, he may be right. If you compare five-year-old boys and five-year-old girls, you won't see much physical difference. They both have the same basic body shape, similar faces and similar voices. They're so similar that in theaters young girls are sometimes cast to play the parts of young boys. In boys' clothing and grooming, audiences can't tell the difference.

Now that you've met Johnny as a five-year-old, let's move time forward. Today Johnny is a teenager. And now we're going to ask him again about girls.

"Are girls pretty, Johnny?"

"Oh, yes," our teenage boy says, "There's just something about them. They look good. They sound good when they talk. They even walk in a cute way. They're really very attractive."

Obviously something has changed. Johnny thinks it's the girls who have changed. And they have indeed changed in certain physical ways. It's no longer easy to costume a teenage girl and let her perform the role of a boy.

But have the girls changed in a way that's really beautiful, or is it Johnny's perception of the girls that makes him feel they are now attractive? How would an independent unbiased observer, not influenced by any human instincts, see the changes in the girls? Let's find out...

Let's try being an unbiased observer and look at the changes that Johnny sees in girls. In order for us to be completely unbiased, let's pretend that we're from out of this world. Just for fun, let's be Martians. We aren't human and we don't have human instincts. We are neither male nor female, and from our sexless condition, we have difficulty telling the human sexes apart. We Martians also have trouble telling the differences between males and females of other earth creatures. Male and female dogs look alike to us Martians. So do male and female cats. Earthlings of the same species all look pretty much alike to us Martians!

24

But as we Martians continue to study these strange earthlings, we notice that some of the humans have changed in their appearance since they were young. The members of one particular group seem a bit distorted. It's the group those humans call "females." Members of this group have wider pelvises that are less well adapted for walking and running, giving them a slightly different gate when they walk. They also have protrusions on their chests that also interfere with their movement. In contrast to those other humans they call "males," they haven't developed much stronger muscles to handle heavy tasks and they haven't grown as large.

Now, as impartial Martians, what would we think of this group? Would we say that the special characteristics of this group are beautiful? Or would we say they appear to us as distortions in the bodies of this one group of humans, not beautiful, not ugly, but certainly of interest in our unbiased study of these strange creatures called humans.

We Martians might find it curious how one human—that teenage human called Johnny—how he reacts to the body changes and distortions of this special group of humans called females.

Girls are great!" teenage Johnny says. "There's something about them that's really cool. They're good-looking. They're pretty!"

But to us Martians, it's obvious that there's something inside teenage Johnny that makes him react so positively to the changes in the females. From our other-world perspective, the females are simply different in certain identifiable ways—not pretty nor ugly to us, just different. The perception of beauty is in Johnny. It's his teenage instincts that tell him, "Yes, the shape of girls' faces and bodies makes them pretty." That's very clear to him because of his instincts, not because of the physical aspects of the teenage girls.

Now suppose we were to say to Johnny, "You're wrong, Johnny. Girls aren't really pretty. It's just your instincts that make you think they're attractive." Johnny would argue vehemently. He would insist, "Can't you see? Girls *are* attractive, it's not just my instincts!" And it's likely that we could never convince Johnny otherwise. Such is the power of our instincts.

Of course, culture complicates things. Where Johnny lives, one item of culture is grooming. The teenage girls around Johnny fix themselves up. They decorate their faces with makeup. They wear nice clothing. They put glittery objects called jewelry on their bodies and hang them from their ears. They trim and arrange the hair on their heads—and remove hair from other places.

Another culture item is girls' behavior. Girls around Johnny do things to attract attention, like talking to the boys, going places where boys go, and girls want to accomplish things that get noticed, like being on the honor roll, running for class office or—dare we hope?—becoming homecoming queen!

The boys' behavior is also part of the culture. Johnny discovers that other boys seem to think girls are something special, and it's hard for him to ignore that peer pressure.

Also, both sexes are exposed to one of our most prominent pieces of culture: advertising. Attraction to the opposite sex is often the main topic of many ads, as well as in movies, television shows and news media.

Yes, culture surrounds Johnny with messages that can influence him powerfully. But it all starts with Johnny's instincts, motivating him to see girls as attractive. Culture can add strength to this effect, as many parents of teenagers will agree. The important point now is that Johnny's teenage instincts are clearly at work.

Now that we've looked at Johnny to see how his instincts drive his perceptions, let's do the same experiment with Jenny, a teenage girl. She, like Johnny, perceives teenage boys according to her instincts. Those instincts tell her that the changes she sees in the boys are attractive, like deeper voices, muscle development and larger size. But we Martians would see things differently. To us aliens, these are only changes, neither pretty nor ugly. Of course, Jenny has a different idea. Jenny is the beholder, and in her eyes, her instincts tell her that boys are pretty "cool." And you can bet that no one will be able to convince her otherwise!

Like most teenagers, Johnny and Jenny are interested in other things besides the opposite sex. For one thing, they like music.

"Strange," we Martians say, "Music is really just organized sounds. It's a kind of noise. But when humans perceive certain sound vibrations, presented in certain combinations, sometimes with a regular pulse these humans call 'rhythm' and certain sequences they call 'melody,' the humans find it pleasant. They sometimes start moving their bodies to match that rhythmic pulse in a ritual they call 'dancing' and they may even use their voices to match the sounds in something they call 'singing.'

"But to us Martians, these are just sounds, not pretty, not ugly, just sounds. We can see that those peculiar humans find these sounds to be pleasant because their instincts tell them so. When we Martians try to tell them that music is neither pretty nor ugly, they disagree instinctively. "

"What's the problem with you Martians," humans say, "Can't you hear it? Can't you feel it? Just listen to that beat. Listen to that melody. That music is pretty. It's not my instincts making me think it's pretty. It's the music."

And there's no convincing them otherwise.

A test for you

Of course, Johnny and Jenny are silly teenagers, too young to recognize how instincts affect them. But you and I are different— aren't we? Can we see the effects of instincts on ourselves? Let's take a test...

Test question number 1: Compare a garter snake and a kitten. Is there a difference in how attractive or ugly these two creatures are? Is one of these uglier than the other? Is one of these more attractive than the other? If your answer is 'yes,' then you're perfectly normal. You are perfectly responding to your instincts.

Your instincts tell you how to perceive a strangely-shaped animal that looks like a piece of wriggling, hissing garden hose with beady eyes and a forked tongue—in contrast to a gently purring four-legged animal with soft fur and wide eyes. You're the beholder. And in your eyes your instincts tell you that a garter snake is not as pretty as a kitten.

If your instincts were not at work, would you see a difference in how attractive these two creatures are? Let's ask a truly unbiased observer, a Martian who doesn't have any of our human instincts...

"No, my fine human," the Martian would say, "I've never seen either of these earth creatures before. To me, neither one is pretty or ugly. They're simply different. It's your human instincts that makes you see the differences as if those differences are in the animals themselves."

27

Test question number 2: You're sitting in a chair by the fireside. One of those pesky Martians walks by and drops a garter snake in your lap. After giving you a few moments to react, the Martian takes away the snake and drops a kitten in your lap. A few moments later the Martin takes away the kitten and asks, "Is there a difference in how scary these two animals are?"

This time your answer is probably a bit more enthusiastic. And you're probably even more upset when the Martian tells you, "The fear you feel is not in the animals. It's in you. It's in your instincts."

The Martian continues, "Think about it. Either one of these creatures could bite you, but neither one is poisonous. Neither one could kill you. Neither one is more scary than the other. Ugly or pretty, scary or not, the difference is not in these two creatures, it's in your perception of them. It's in your instincts."

Grading your test

Now let's grade your test. Did you find that attractiveness or scariness is a characteristic of the snake and the kitten, not of your instincts? If so, you're a normal, typical human. After all, we're not really Martians. We humans have great difficulty stepping out from under the influence of our instincts and seeing them at work inside us. It's very hard for us to see how our instincts direct the way we see things—the way we see everything. When we feel emotions like joy, disappointment, pleasure or sorrow, we are really feeling our instincts at work.

Things that surround us are neither good nor bad, pretty nor ugly. It's our instincts that put these values on things, not the things themselves. When the brain is exposed to something, the instinctive patterns in the brain generate a reaction that may say, "This is something I want" or "I'm afraid of that." To the brain, these are factual ideas. Instincts have told it so.

Are instincts the whole story?

Being motivated by instincts doesn't mean there's anything wrong with us. That, in fact, is how we work. Instincts shape the perceptions that guide our actions. And that's the simple process by which we humans have accomplished great things.

Of course, our perceptions are not determined by instincts alone. Culture also plays a part. That loud motorcycle exhaust may not be disturbing to a person who has learned to work on motorcycles. That weird abstract painting may be beautiful to an art student who has learned to appreciate abstract composition. That distorted monster face may not be scary to a person who has learned it's merely a mask for a Halloween party. Cooked snails may not be repulsive to a person who has developed an acquired taste for escargot.

Learning is culture, and it can change our perceptions. That's why we have teachers. That's why we value the human institutions that we've learned to build. And learning about garter snakes could change how attractive or scary they are. Our perceptions are based on instincts, but shaped by culture.

Perhaps we can replace the saying that started this chapter and say,

Beauty is in the instincts and culture of the beholder.

We'll talk more about culture in a later chapter.

Animals of all classes, old and young, shrink with instinctive fear from any strange object approaching them.

—William Henry Hudson

Chapter 6
Misconceptions

To properly understand our instincts, we have to clear up some confusing but popular ideas about what instincts are.

Misconception Number 1: Instincts are *reflexes*.

No, instincts are not reflexes.

A *reflex* is an action we take without any conscious thought. The brain isn't involved in a reflex. The classic example is the knee-jerk reaction. A doctor lightly taps on your knee so as to strike the patellar tendon in your knee. Your lower leg immediately jerks in a kicking motion. You didn't think about it. The doctor's tap sent a signal that automatically tensed the muscles to jerk your leg. That's a reflex.

Put a peppermint drop in your mouth and you'll begin to salivate. That's another reflex. No thought was involved. Make a sudden move toward a person's face and he/she will blink. These reactions are often described as instinctive, but they are not instincts. They are reflexes.

Misconception Number 2: Instincts are *intuition*.

No, instincts are not intuition.

Intuition is very often confused with instincts. Here's the difference:

• *Instincts* are purely genetically-based. They are our built-in motivators that drive everything we do. We can't change them or remove them.

• *Intuition* includes the effect of our culture, of our learning.

Let's look at some examples of how intuition can be confused with instinct. You may hear comments like these:

• "The baseball player *instinctively* threw the ball to third base instead of to home plate."

• "The soldier *instinctively* saluted when he saw the general."

• "I can *instinctively* recognize a fellow Italian."

No, these are not instinctive actions. They are intuitive. Intuition involves culture; that is, some learning, some knowledge. A baseball player knows a lot about throwing a ball and how the game is played, so his action is intuitive, not instinctive. A soldier knows how to salute and knows there are consequences if he fails to salute a general, so his salute is intuitive, not instinctive. A person who grew up around Italians knows Italian culture and may be able to recognize even tiny traces of it, such as mannerisms, doing so by intuition, not instinct.

Intuition is commonly confused with instinct. They are not the same thing.

Misconception Number 3: Instincts are uncontrollable.

No, our reaction to instincts can be controlled.

It's commonly thought that instincts cannot be resisted, that an instinctive urge generates a reaction that no amount of will power can modify or avoid. Not so, according to the way we are defining instincts here.

There are differences in the strength of our instincts. Some are quite powerful and seemingly impossible to resist. But no matter how strong, culture can modify how an instinct is expressed. For example, anger is a rather strong instinct. It's hard to resist retaliating to a powerful hurt or a dramatic loss. Imagine the reaction of a mother whose child is snatched from her arms. She may fight back desperately, perhaps even risking her own safety in trying to stop the abduction. That's the effect of a strong instinct: the instinct to protect one's young.

Some instincts are weaker and are easier to control through culture. For example, imagine the reaction of that same woman who fought desperately when her child was taken from her. In this example, she hasn't experienced the loss of her child. Instead, imagine that she has spent several hours preparing a supper that she hopes will please her family. When they sit down to eat, they nibble at the food and say nothing to indicate they appreciate all of her time and effort. She may say nothing about it, being unsure at that moment how to deal with her disappointment of a less strong instinct: the instinct for human acceptance and companionship. She's controlling her reaction to that instinct.

Before going on to learn more about how our instincts work, let's clear up a possible misunderstanding: Here, instincts are defined as genetically-based motivations. That's a broad category, and it includes every human activity. And that's a good way for us to understand what's going on in our behavior. However, psychologists often make further classifications, like separating motivations from emotions. That's okay, and it doesn't really conflict with our definition of instincts. It's just a different way to look at the same subject.

What is the basis of our instincts?

Survival is the basis of all of our instincts. Our ancestors who gave us our instincts were survivors. They were motivated to overcome obstacles and dangers that threatened their existence. If they had not triumphed over these challenges, they would not have become our ancestors. In contrast, many of their friends, neighbors and enemies did not survive. But every one of our ancestors did survive, no matter how far back you trace our lineage. We are the children of survivors. We have their survival instinct.

Here's another important fact about our ancestors: Every one of them also reproduced. Not one of them failed to reproduce him/herself. If they had merely survived over challenges like famine, wars and animal attacks, but had not reproduced, those survival instincts would have died with them. Reproduction is a key part of survival.

So we now possess the instincts for survival and reproduction of our ancestors, passed down to us by individuals who, without exception, were all completely successful at surviving and reproducing. Yes, we are entitled to be proud: Our mommies and daddies and grannies and gramps and ancestors all the way back were all winners. And we all have their winning instincts. Yay, us!

Now, when you see anyone walking down the street, playing with a kid, tossing around a ball, reading a book or doing absolutely anything, you can be sure you are watching a winner. You're watching someone who is motivated by the instinct to survive. And every action of that person is motivated by that survival instinct.

If we wanted to write a movie script to show the strongest of all human instincts, we might do something like this:

A man is walking through the park. Suddenly, a large monster appears and roars at him. It's a talking monster, and it says, "I'm going to attack you and kill you!" The man grabs a nearby stick and begins to strike the monster, all the time screaming for help to other people around him. The man tries to run away, but the monster blocks his path. The man uses every weapon he can find and every tactic he can think of to fight off the monster. He's fighting for his life...

Our screenplay shows a person motivated by the most basic of all instincts, the instinct for survival. What this man wants most—and what each of us wants most of all—is to survive, to continue to live. Everything we do, no matter how trivial, is motivated by this survival instinct on some level.

Now, for the sake of a happy ending, the man in the park suddenly remembers he has a package of dog food in his pocket. He throws it toward the monster. The monster stops his attacks and eats the dog food while the man escapes. The music comes up, the credits roll and the film ends.

Luckily, in our day-to-day experiences, we don't meet monsters and we may never feel that our life is threatened. But we think about our next meal, about the loyalty of our friends, about how we're doing in our job—all of which are related to our survival.

Our simple ordinary everyday activities are all somehow aimed at survival. Unlike other living things, we humans can't base our survival on having claws, sharp teeth, warm fur or other natural protections. Nature has left us naked, without weapons and without other implements to help us survive.

A lone human, dropped into a forest empty handed, would not have much chance of survival. We'd need help: some warm clothes, some fishing tackle or another way to catch food, a shelter of some kind, maybe even a Boy Scout manual on wilderness living. These are the kinds of things modern campers take into the woods so they can survive comfortably. They're also the kinds of things city dwellers have readily at hand, just down the street or over at the shopping mall.

Can you spot what all these tools for survival have in common? All of them—everything we use daily for our own survival—all of it is produced by other humans or learned from other humans. Yes, indeed, we're all in this together.

34

We humans are social animals, surviving by helping each other. Our clothing is made by other people using materials and techniques developed by other people. Our food is produced using agricultural techniques developed over many years by other people.

We're all extremely interdependent, relying on each other for the tools and the knowledge we need to survive. Even a lone hermit, living completely alone in the woods, survives by using what he got from other humans: things like the concepts of wearing protective clothing, using tools and weapons, and distinguishing between friend and foe. That hermit may not like to be around other people, but he's as dependent on them as any of us are.

You can see that our basic tool for survival is other people. As a result, we have finely-developed *social instincts*. We pay attention to other people. We befriend them. We seek to be accepted by them. We want to work with them.

We seek to be close to other people. Around the world, people are moving away from remote rural locations to concentrate more and more in cities.

We learn from other people. We have an expanding worldwide industry of education consisting of schools, institutes, communication media, industrial training and, yes, even advertising.

We often refer to our professional work as "earning a living." Some people refer to the money they earn as "bread." Perhaps without realizing it, we already recognize that everything we do is somehow related to survival.

The instinct to survive is human nature itself, and every aspect of our personalities derives from it.

—Robert A. Heinlein, Starship Troopers

Chapter 7
Sex

Now we come to the part of this book that you've probably been waiting for: the part about sex. Sex is an interesting topic, but that's not why we're going to talk about it. Not because it's interesting. We'll do it because sex is one of the best examples of our instincts in action. With this good example under our belts, we'll be better able to understand how our other less interesting instincts motivate us.

Remember that all of our instincts are aimed at helping us to survive. Our survival instinct comes in many forms. The two principal forms are: 1) Our instinct *to survive threats* like an animal attack, a food shortage or some other sort of catastrophe; and 2) Our instinct *to reproduce*. Both of these try for survival, though they do it in different ways. We saw the instinct to survive against threats in our made-up movie monster attack in the previous chapter. Now we'll see how our reproduction instinct motivates us to survive in our everyday lives.

The reproduction instinct is strong.

We all spend a lot of time and energy on reproduction. It's one of the things that matters most to us. We include details of our children in our resumes and our biographies. When older people are asked to talk about their lives, they typically start by proudly describing their children and grandchildren, sometimes at great length. When young people are asked to describe their goals in life, they often include the desire for a family, meaning, of course, to have children.

You are the descendant of individuals who were strongly motivated to reproduce. Every one of your ancestors reproduced. Yes, every one of them! Your mother and father, your grandparents, your great-great-great—umpteen greats grandparents all reproduced. Going back however far you want into your ancestry, you won't find even one individual who didn't reproduce.

Your maiden aunt and your bachelor uncle didn't reproduce. They didn't leave any biological trace of their existence in the world.

They may have accomplished great things and may have been greatly admired, but once their lives were over, they were no longer physically represented in the human race.

That's why our instinct to reproduce is so strong. Reproducing is absolutely necessary for our survival as a human race. Those ancestors who chose to reproduce themselves have configured the human race as it is now.

We pay attention to sex.

Since we humans reproduce by sex, instincts related to sex are paramount. Suppose you were told, "You should meet a person on the southeast corner of Main and Elm Streets at 2 p.m. today." Now what's the first question you would ask? How about: "Is the person I'm meeting a man or a woman?"

We strongly categorize people by their sex. Our sexual identity is so strong that we use special names for each sex, as if their sex were their total identity. We don't refer to them as "male people" and "female people." Instead we give them names as if their sex totally described them. We call them "men" and "women." Maleness and femaleness is only one aspect of them, but we treat it as a complete description.

We emphasize our sex by constantly wearing the appropriate uniform for male and female. We decorate and groom ourselves to add further sexual emphasis. In Western culture, male humans typically wear simplified clothing, often without much decoration or jewelry. Some of them cultivate moustaches and beards to emphasize their maleness. Meanwhile, the female humans generally wear more decorative clothing than the males, sometimes including skirts, artistically-designed shoes and other adornments and jewelry. The females paint their faces and some punch holes in their ear lobes on which to hang ornaments.

That's what we in our Western culture do to make us look female or male. But cultures around the world have their own uniforms for their sex. Women in African cultures have sometimes used piles of rings to stretch their necks. They've distended their ear lobes and pierced their faces. Certain Chinese women were once crippled by having their feet bound so they would grow unusually small. Men in some cultures have scarred their faces to be distinctive. In some cultures the males cut their hair short and the females grow it long. In other cultures it's the other way around: the females cut their hair short and the males grow it long. The need to be identified with one's sex is obviously universal and strong. It's instinctive.

Sex is everywhere.

We pay a lot of attention to sex. It's a common theme in our literature and in theater and other forms of art. We have lots of love stories: Romeo and Juliet, Cleopatra and Mark Antony, Scarlett O'Hara and Rhett Butler—even Mickey and Minnie Mouse.

Movies nearly always include a boy/girl romance, whether it's the major focus of the script as in *Sleepless in Seattle*, or a side plot to the major story as in *Star Wars*, or an incidental aspect of the movie as in *The Right Stuff*.

Many of the popular television shows use love stories or other sorts of sexual tension to hold our attention, and TV advertising uses sexual themes to sell perfume, razors, clothing, exercise devices and beer.

Sex is in language.

When we speak, we pay strict attention to sex. This is our reproductive instinct at work, motivating us to pay attention to whatever is male and female.

In various languages, sex is an essential part of grammar. We English speakers say "him" and "her" when we could be saying "it" to refer to another human. Sex is so ingrained in our language that we would find it uncomfortable to talk about the arrival of Uncle George by saying, "It walked into a room and greeted its friends." Uncle George might be offended, even though he technically is an "it."

We even insist on referring to our animals by their sex, calling our dogs and cats "he" and "she" when we often can't see the difference.

We sometimes attribute sex to objects that very obviously don't have sex. We pretend that big transportation vessels like ships and airliners are female. Sailors typically refer to their ships as "she," the same way airline pilots sometimes refer to their airplanes.

Even though there's lots of sex talk in our English. it's one of the least sexy languages. Other languages are much sexier. Like English, European languages also use sex-defined pronouns. The English "he" and "she" become "el" and "ella" in Spanish, and the same thing happens in French, Spanish, German and other languages. But in these other languages, the sex talk goes even further. For example, in Spanish nearly everything has sex, including inanimate objects. A table is female (*la mesa*), a door is male (*el puerto*). In French, a car is female (la *voiture*), a bike is male (*le vélo*).

Sex is obviously instinctive.

Sex just *feels* like some kind of an instinct. Sex is really irrational, isn't it? What rational person would spend so many hours of that person's life seeking a mate, primping and searching and studying the target sex? And once that target mate is found, the actual act of reproduction is quite undignified, so much so that it's typically conducted away from public view.

Then, having succeeded in producing an offspring, the parents must spend enormous portions of their time, energy and money catering to the needs of their progeny, usually to the neglect of their own needs.

For females, reproduction is a big ordeal. There are nine months of discomfort, morning sickness, a distorted body, unflattering clothes, a sore back. Then comes the delivery. Until recent times the act of childbirth was dangerous and sometimes fatal. Now things are better. In the United States we still lose one or two mothers per 10,000 births*. Even with that somber prospect, we eagerly march to the tune of our instinct to reproduce.

Viewed rationally, it's hard to see why we humans would want to reproduce. There's nothing in it to benefit us, is there?

The answer to that question usually comes quickly. "We *want* the joy of raising children," we usually say. "We *love* our children. We *feel* good seeing them grow up."

Maternal Mortality in 2005. Estimates by WHO (World Health Organization), UNICEF (United Nations Children's Fund), UNFPA (United Nations Population Fund) and The World Bank.

Do those sound like rational reasons? No. Words like "want," "love" and "feel" are expressing *emotions*. Not rational reasons, *emotions*. And, as we've seen, emotions are the tools of our instincts. It's our instincts that are motivating us to reproduce. And since sex is the way we reproduce, we continue to follow the clarian call of our instincts!

Sex is more than reproduction.

It should be simple to see how sex contributes to our survival, the goal of all our instincts. Sex reproduces us. But there's another way sex helps us to survive: by motivating pair bonding. Our sex instincts motivate two individuals to unite, not just temporarily, as with some animals, but for a longer term. The brain chemicals that we generate during sexual activity include oxytocin and other hormones that produce a feeling of love and bonding between the two participants. This motivates both parents to remain together for a longer term, hopefully long enough to nurture their offspring.

It's no news to the parents among us that human babies require *lots* of care! Our newborns arrive in a very undeveloped condition, almost entirely unable to look out for themselves. This is very different from some animals such as horses and cows. These animal babies are so fully mature when born that within minutes they make wobbly attempts to stand up, and soon succeed in walking around. Not so with our own newborns, who can barely perform even the most simple acts of self sufficiency.

By our human bonding through sex, we provide a two-parent protective unit for our immature babies, giving them a much better chance of growing up and thereby contributing to our survival.

So this is how instincts work...

Now you've seen how our instinct to reproduce works. It's really aimed at survival, the goal of all our instincts. And it's a very strong instinct. But there are other instincts that are much less obvious, also aimed at survival. For example, we have instincts for social acceptance, to feed ourselves, to solve problems, to analyze the world around us. We constantly feel the pull of our instincts. We'll soon discuss more of these other instincts.

*The human instinct for self-preservation is strong.
You have the right to self-defense. You have the right
to survive, if you can.*

                            —Nancy Werlin, The Rules of Survival

Chapter 8

The Nature of Our Nature

To this point, we've been introduced to our instincts. We've talked about what they are: motivating forces inherited from our ancestors that drive us in everything we do. They're with us in our every thought and action. Without them, we'd never do anything. We'd never survive.

That makes them very important, doesn't it? After all, we spend our lives working to satisfy our instincts. From the moment of our birth when we take our first breath, our instincts are driving us to learn how to fulfill our instincts' demands. To do that, we spend our lives acquiring culture.

That's what culture is—all the things we can find and invent to meet the wants of our instincts. Pursuing culture to satisfy our instincts is what we do throughout our lives. That's *all* we do.

So, the more we know about our instincts, the better able we'll be to understand ourselves—and everyone around us.

From here on, we're going to talk about what our instincts are like. We're going to describe their nature. We're going to see what they look like when they're stripped of the culture that we've created to satisfy them.

Selfish instincts

When you take away the effects of culture, all of our instincts have one thing in common: they're entirely selfish. Yes, selfish. Entirely. But how's this possible?

As we've discussed before, the goal of our instincts is survival. And survival is a selfish thing. Like your ancestors before you, you have to take care of yourself. In a contest, your ancestors had to win. If there wasn't enough food, the one who took it was the one who survived. If there was danger, the one who defeated it was the one who survived. If there was competition for a mate, the one who got the mate was the one who became your ancestor.

Since everything we do is motivated by our instincts, at an instinctive level everything we do is basically selfish.

This idea may be hard to take for many of us. We're not used to thinking of ourselves as basically selfish. But consider this: Why do we root for the home team? Because we identify with the home team and we selfishly want to be winners. Why do we want the best possible education for our kids? Because we selfishly want our kids to have every possible advantage.

There are even simpler examples: Why do we go to the grocery store? Because we selfishly want to feed ourselves. Why do we sit down and read a book? Because we selfishly want to entertain ourselves or learn something.

Why do we do anything? Because we want to. If we didn't want to, we wouldn't do anything. And what we choose to do, we always choose on a fundamentally selfish basis.

Don't we sometimes do things we don't want to do?

What if we're forced to do something? Are we still choosing something we want?

Let's take an extreme example: A thief runs up to you, points a gun at you, and says, "Give me all your money!"

You don't want to give the thief all your money, do you? But do you give it to him? Yes. And why? Because you've made the choice that you would rather give him your money than risk being shot. You made a selfish decision to survive. Good for you!

Maybe not everyone would make that decision. The comedian Jack Benny, who was famous for his penny-pinching ways, sometimes joked about the situation of the thief with a gun. The thief says, "Your money or your life!" Jack Benny says, "I'm thinking, I'm thinking."

But let's take another example. What about those mornings when you really didn't want to get up and go to your job? Or you really didn't want to go with a friend to the opera? Or you really didn't want to entertain your mother-in-law on her next visit? Did you make a selfish decision?

If you decided to go to work, sit through the opera or smile for your mother-in-law, it's because you decided that course of action was the best for you. You didn't want to risk losing your job. You didn't want to risk offending your friend by not going to the opera.

You didn't want to offend your mother-in-law by not entertaining her. In every case, you chose what's best for you. You made a selfish decision.

Selfish genes and selfish instincts

Since instincts are genetic, that is, inherited through our DNA, it's not surprising that our instincts are like our DNA. And if you ask the scientists, our DNA is entirely selfish.

In his groundbreaking book first published in 1976, *The Selfish Gene*, zoologist Richard Dawkins set out a view that is now well established in the scientific community, that the nature we inherit is utterly selfish:

> *"...if you wish, as I do, to build a society in which individuals cooperate generously and unselfishly towards a common good, you can expect little help from biological nature...we are born selfish."*

Scientists' view of our selfish nature is easy to see in a newborn infant. The baby human cries whenever it wants something. It pays attention only to its own needs. It's entirely selfish, as many tired and sleepy parents can confirm.

As the baby grows and matures, it learns to pay attention to the needs of others. Its parents teach the young child, "Don't be selfish. Learn to share." The child discovers that if you cooperate and help other people, there are rewards. The child is learning culture, and culture makes it harder and harder to see the underlying selfish instincts.

But what about altruism?

Sometimes we do really nice things, altruistic things that seem to be for the benefit of others. Are these things selfish? Consider one of the prime principles of altruism, The Golden Rule:

> *"Do unto others as you would have them do unto you."*

If we follow this rule, as many of us strive to do, why do we do it? Let's interview someone who believes in this Golden Rule...

Q: "Why do you treat people according to The Golden Rule?"

A: "I do it because I think everyone should be treated that way."

Q: "What way?"

A: " The way I would like to be treated."

Q: "Who decided how you would like to be treated?

A: "I did."

Q: "Why do you treat them this way?"

A: "Because I think that's the way it should be."

Q: "Why?"

A: "Because that's what I want."

Does this look like a selfish decision? Working to make the world the way one wants it to be? While one's view of good behavior may be very commendable, the decision in this case appears to be made on a selfish basis: One wants things to be a certain way, one's own way.

What about the heroes?

We love the stories about a hero who rushed into a burning building to rescue an elderly woman. Or a man who donated his kidney to a complete stranger. Or a soldier who threw himself on a live grenade to save his buddies. All are very commendable acts, and we'd all probably agree that these heroes deserve the awards, recognition and medals we like to give them.

We'd all probably agree that this is true altruism—as true as it gets. But even in these situations, at a basic level our selfish instincts are always at work. In the moment of decision to commit the heroic act, our heroes make a choice. Very often it's to perform according to a learned pattern, a pattern that says, "This is the way I think things should be."

There's a pattern in our culture that says it's right to run into a burning building to save someone in distress, it's right to donate a kidney to someone in need, and since that live grenade is about to go off and kill me, it's right to fall on it and save my buddies. These heroes choose what they think is the right course of action. They do things the way they want them to be in that situation. They do what they want.

46

Sometimes people openly sacrifice themselves. During World War II, Kamikaze pilots flew airplanes loaded with explosives into ships of their enemies and died in the blast. Islamic suicide bombers have set off explosive vests in crowded places to terrorize the population. Christians in ancient Rome sacrificed themselves before hungry wild animals.

It's hard to see how selfish motivation could bring a person to willingly sacrifice him/herself. But these people believed some positive reward was waiting that would be worth the sacrifice— martyrdom, recognition, or perhaps some grand glory to be received in a life after death. In some cases the alternative to death was a life of unbearable abuse or abhorrent treatment, and self-destruction became the preferred choice.

In each of these cases the underlying instinct is a selfish one. But in each case, culture plays a role in addition to the influence of instinct. Culture can teach us that it's right to sacrifice oneself for a person in distress, or for a greater good such as a victory in war, or for the glory of one's deity. Culture can overcome the instinct for self preservation and make self sacrifice the preferable alternative.

What we can learn from dogs

Dogs are instinctive creatures. In that, they're very much like us. And they behave in a manner that seems very unselfish. They follow their keepers around, sitting when they're told to "Sit," rolling over on command and generally doing whatever their keepers want.

This may look like unselfish behavior, but it's not. Like people, dogs have instincts that are totally selfish. In doing all these seemingly unselfish things, dogs are expressing the instincts that humans have selected in them. Over the ages, people selected the dogs that behaved in ways their keepers liked. By following those instincts to please their keepers, dogs survived—a purely selfish act.

Dogs are entirely created by humans. They are the descendents of wolves. Over the centuries, people discovered that certain individual wolves had instincts that were more friendly with humans. When people selected these wolves and they had pups, the people again selected the ones with the instincts they preferred. Eventually the result was different enough to be given a new name, a "dog." By this time, it had the instincts that were preferred by humans, including the tendency to be submissive to humans, to "love its master." For a dog, this is an entirely selfish instinct, since it allows the animal to survive.

Even though behavior may look unselfish, it's all motivated by selfish instincts, whether it's man or beast!

Thoughts on being selfish

At an early age, most of us are taught that it's bad to be selfish. Sharing is one of the lessons of kindergarten. Teamwork is emphasized in work and play. Most of us would feel insulted if someone accused us of being "selfish."

And that's good, isn't it? Our culture has determined that we can do better working together. A group that cooperates can build cities and universities and public parks. Sports teams that work well together can win games. Nations whose individual citizens collaborate can achieve prosperity for all its people.

Our culture recognizes that we're social creatures, and the better we are at being social, the more we can accomplish. Culture can take our selfish instincts and channel them into great success. Business schools teach the motto, "All of us are better than one of us."

We needn't fret about having selfish instincts. When our selfish instincts are combined with our social culture, we have a powerful combination. One of the tenets of democracy is "enlightened *self* interest," which holds that if we act to further the interests of others, ultimately we serve our own self-interest. We value "*self* reliance," being "*self* motivated," having "*self* esteem" and "*self* determination."

There's nothing wrong with being motivated by selfish instincts in everything we do. We're stuck with these instincts anyway, since they're in our DNA. And for our ancestors, these instincts served them well. That's how *we* got here!

Chapter 9
The Final Chapter

You've seen final chapters before. This the place where the author sums up the ideas of the book in a few simple words. Then the author tells you in plain language why he/she took the time to write all of this. Then the author signs off with thoughts about the future and what's in it for you.

Since we're about to cover all of that, it makes this the final chapter of this book. And though we're calling this the *final* chapter, it's not the *last* chapter. If you look ahead, you can see that there's more to this book, and it's pretty good stuff.

Coming up, you'll find examples of specific human instincts. Some of these have been extensively studied by scientists. The list also includes possible instincts; that is, things that appear to be instincts but that haven't been studied enough to be sure about them.

In the remaining pages you'll see that this isn't the first book about human nature and human instincts. People have been puzzling over the way we people think and act for centuries, trying to figure out what we're all about. This book is another step in understanding what we're all about.

At the back of this book you'll also find a list of other books that you may want to read. We might call this a "bibliography," but that's not the best name for what I'll call a "book list." Besides, the books aren't listed here in the classic bibliography format, since today you can easily find any of them in an internet search. These are really just good books, and they're some of the sources of information for what you're reading here. I want to encourage you to read some of them, whichever ones may interest you. They can help you understand what we're talking about here, and you can learn lots of other interesting things.

Summing up the ideas

Let's boil down our discussion to its bare essence. Here's a concise statement of what we've been talking about:

We all have it. Every one of us. It's the force within us. It's our instincts, motivating everything we do, every minute, every day of our lives.

We're born with our instincts. They're designated by our DNA and handed down from our ancestors. We're stuck with them. It's doubtful we can ever change our instincts.

Our instincts work by giving us emotions which we experience as feelings. All of our emotions are generated by our instincts.

Although we can't change our instincts, we can use our culture to change how we respond to them. That, in fact, is what we do throughout our lives. Essentially all human behavior is a mixture of instincts and culture. Instincts motivate us, culture directs how we respond to our instincts.

So what?

We need to understand our instincts because we need to understand people. We humans, the most social creatures known, rely earnestly on other people. Together we're the most powerful creatures known to exist. Separately we're naked, weak, poorly-adapted individuals destined to be driven to extinction by the rest of the kingdom of life.

This book is drawn from many other attempts to understand what makes people tick—our human nature. You'll find many of these ideas in the book list that's printed here. The book you have in your hands is a digest of those ideas condensed into one simple scientific model. Nothing in the books of our list seems to refute this model.

What's a scientific model? It's a tool used by scientists to figure things out. For example, consider the atom. No one has ever seen an atom. Yet, scientists can tell us in great detail what an atom looks like: little protons and neutrons stuck together in a nucleus with teensy electrons orbiting around outside.

How did scientists figure that out? They couldn't look through a microscope; an atom is way too small for that. Instead, they constructed a model. They looked at how matter behaves and made an educated estimate of what must be in an atom. Then they did experiments to see if they were right. Eventually, after enough experiments, they decided that, yes, the model is right.

That's what we have here: a model of our instincts and how they fit together with our culture to produce the baffling behavior of us humans. It fits the observations of many learned people, and it's the result of seven decades of study by Yours Truly, the author. And I want to share this idea with you.

What's in this for you?

Imagine a world in which we understood our instincts. In this world we would have a complete understanding of what nature is telling us to do. And in this world we could develop a culture that satisfies our instincts simply and completely. Wouldn't that be wonderful?

Is that an impossible dream? Not really. We're already working on it. Since our human race began, we people have been trying to figure out how to satisfy our instincts. In fact, that's exactly what we're doing every day, in every waking moment, in every action we take. Our instincts tell us what we want and we work to get whatever our instincts tell us.

The trouble is, we're doing it the hard way, by trial and error. We develop things and see if they satisfy some instinct. Some of these things work well, some of them don't. We keep the things that satisfy our instincts. We discard the things that don't. Little by little, we make progress with those things. The things we develop are our culture.

If you look back at our human history you can see the immense progress we've made. Our ancestors weren't always very good at providing food, clothing and shelter for everyone. Sometimes they went hungry. Sometimes they starved. Today our culture does a much better job, so good that, in some countries, obesity is a much bigger problem than starvation.

Our ancestors had to constantly fight over things they needed. If a person planted an apple tree, he had to keep away others who might come and steal his fruit. Today we have laws that recognize the concept of possession. And we have police to enforce those laws. Laws and possession are culture.

Look around. Everywhere you can see our culture, built piece by piece to satisfy our instincts. This trial-and-error process has produced impressive progress.

But advancement like this has been extremely slow and messy. While our instincts have been constantly motivating us, the things we've tried in our culture to satisfy them have often been wasteful and harmful. Some of the most obviously unproductive things we've developed are wars and weapons, intended to satisfy instincts such as those for possession, conflict and control. Another unproductive piece of culture is religious and racial persecution, intended to satisfy instincts such as those for social order.

These are obviously terrible cultural developments, but it's really hard to resist our instincts to do these kinds of things. Someone's instincts said that capturing another country would be a good thing, or eliminating someone else's "false beliefs" would improve people's lives. And someone else's instincts motivated him/ her to fight back, to wage a counter war, to extract revenge and to seek "justice."

We would have a better chance of avoiding these terrible cultural ideas if we understood our instincts and developed productive, positive cultural ideas instead. We may be making progress in moving ahead, but it's taking a long, long time for us to evolve into better methods of satisfying our instincts.

Wouldn't it be better if we first understood our instincts? Couldn't we come up with better, more effective ways to satisfy our instincts if we knew better what was motivating us?

That's what this book is all about.

We are survival machines - robot vehicles blindly programmed to preserve the selfish molecules known as genes.

—Richard Dawkins, The Selfish Gene

I've been reading some philosophy - everybody seems to agree that the instinct and responsibility of all humans is to take care of themselves first.
                    —Nancy Werlin, The Rules of Survival

Chapter 10
A Short but Complete List of Our Instincts

At last you can see a complete list of all our human instincts! In this chapter we'll cover the entire subject, and we'll do it extremely quickly and simply. This shortest possible list of human instincts is the most complete one. Here it is:

Survival

This is our whole set of instincts, all wrapped up into one. It could be said that we really only have one instinct: survival. All the other things we describe as instincts are manifestations of this basic instinct. We constantly strive to survive, to win, to excel, to stay alive. Over our long history we've developed many instinctive urges to accomplish this objective, all aimed directly or indirectly at our survival. We'll discuss many of them in the next chapter.

The goal of all our instincts is self preservation. Therefore, our instincts are, in their pure form, entirely selfish. It's our culture that produces our more noble and less selfish characteristics. The survival instinct is described more fully in Chapters 6 and 8.

Reproduction

This might be considered our second most important instinct. After our survival instinct motivates us to survive all challenges, we must reproduce so that we may survive in the persons of our progeny. Without reproduction, all of our physical existence is forever lost. Every one of our ancestors reproduced, and we have inherited this instinct from them.

It's easy to see the reproduction instinct. Reproduction is the focus of many people's life goals of home and family. It's a feature on resumes. It fascinates genealogy fans. It's a factor in forecasts of economists. It's a popular topic of conversation. This reproduction instinct is described more fully in Chapter 7.

You now have a shockingly short and complete list of our instincts. But to really understand ourselves in a way that can help us in our daily lives, you'll probably want to know more. You'll find that detail in the next chapter.

*Human nature is potentially aggressive and destructive
and potentially orderly and constructive.*

—*Margaret Mead*

Chapter 11
A Long but Incomplete List of Our Instincts

Here's where we get to the really useful, really interesting information about our instincts. This chapter begins breaking up our survival and reproduction instincts into more specific instincts. The force within us comes in many instinctive urges, many of which have been deeply researched and documented and which are well established among scholars.

There are other instincts within us that are not yet well established. We'll include a few of these probable instincts. And there are undoubtedly many more instincts yet to be defined and studied. As the study of human instincts proceeds, we can expect to see many more ideas presented that could be added to the list.

Where do we start?

Feel free to skim through this chapter, reading about whatever instincts seem interesting to you. Or read them all, since every one provides food for thought. To help you, there's an index of these instincts on page 81.

This long list isn't the first one of its type. This monumental task has been pursued for centuries by many people. One grand effort was made by Donald E. Brown, a professor of anthropology who worked at the University of California, Santa Barbara. He published a long list of human universals; that is, things found in all humans everywhere. There were more than 300 items in his original list, and after it was published in 1991, he added many more. Here are some examples of what he put into his list:

Human Universals

aesthetics	music
baby talk	poetry/rhetoric
conflict	property
government	reciprocity
hairstyles	tools
jokes	taking turns
leaders	weapons

and more than 300 more...

Donald Brown said that the items in his list "comprise those features of culture, society, language, behavior, and psyche for which there are no known exceptions." His goal was to describe human nature, not just instincts. He didn't distinguish between the effects of instincts and the effects of culture. However, instincts are involved in each of the features he listed. For example, hairstyles are motivated, at least partially, by the instinct for social acceptance. But there's plenty of culture in a haircut and set!

Now, undaunted by the immensity of the task, we will soldier on in our quest to list our human instincts. Our list will be considerably shorter than the 300-plus items of Professor Brown.

As we look at this list, we're examining human instincts at a time when there's still much, much more to be learned about them. In the future we'll all understand our instincts — and ourselves — much better.

Our list of instincts

Here's a preview of what's in this chapter:

Sex	Acquisition/Possession
Fear	Male and female instincts
Anger	Social instincts
Violence	Social acceptance
	Gregariousness
Order	Recognition of one's own kind
Patterns/Causality	Friend and foe
Reciprocity	Protection of children
	Search for a leader
Conflict	Aesthetics
Language	Facial recognition
Morality	Music
Spirituality	Rhyme

Sex

Since we humans reproduce by sex, our sexual instinct is prominent. It occupies much of our time and effort. It's ever present in our language, art, social activities and throughout our culture. The sex instinct works by making our target sex (generally the opposite sex) appear attractive to us. Without this instinct, our target sex would seem no more attractive than our non-target sex (generally our own sex). Sex also encourages pair bonding, providing our offspring with two parents to nurture our very immature newborns and to protect them as they grow up. As a result of our parenting, our offspring can mature and do their own reproducing. This sex instinct is described more fully in Chapters 5 and 7.

Fear

The fear instinct can produce a very strong feeling. Fear can be triggered by lots of things. We instinctively fear loud noises, we fear roaring sounds like racing engines and animal cries, we fear things that are large like big animals and huge machines and monsters in movies, we fear fast-moving objects and unfamiliar situations.

We have lots of phobias, like claustrophobia (fear of closed places, acrophobia (fear of heights), and countless more such as octophobia (fear of the figure 8).

In these phobias, the emotional force of our instincts overpowers our more rational understanding. For example, imagine a claustrophobic person who's standing in front of an elevator feeling the emotional force of a fear instinct. Could that person overcome her fear by a rational explanation that the elevator has been carefully engineered and tested and is extremely unlikely to fail? Not likely.

Or how about an acrophobic person who's feeling the force of fear before boarding an airplane. Could that person be comforted by a rational explanation of the principles of lift and the solid characteristics of "thin air?" It's doubtful. Our instincts can produce a very strong emotional force, strong enough to defy the rational ideas that our culture provides.

Anger

Anger is one of our strongest instincts. It produces a very potent emotion that can be difficult to resist. When triggered, anger seems to take over the mind and body, suppressing rational thought and stimulating aggressive action. We often describe an angry person as being "mad." In its extreme, anger can cause persons to do things he/she would never do in a calmer state, including self-destructive acts.

Anthropologists believe that anger is a protective survival instinct. When we observe an angry person, we tend to stay away from him/her, suspecting that the "mad" person may do something extreme and destructive.

Anger works like the legendary doomsday machine. That's the fabled machine that a country might build to protect itself. The doomsday machine would be able to destroy everything including the country itself. It would be set to go off automatically if the country were attacked. As a result, any country that wanted to attack would know that it, too, would be destroyed if it attacked. Thus, the doomsday machine would serve as a protection.

Anger is similar. An angry person may appear to be ready to take aggressive action against everyone and everything, including him/herself. This can provide some protection by discouraging aggression by others. And this can lead to survival, the goal of all instincts.

Violence

Grit your teeth. Here comes the nastiest of the instincts in this list. Violence may be the most graphic example of a force within us. Ugly as it is, we're attracted by violence. That's what draws us to many movies, video games and books. And in a more muted form, it attracts us to many sports, such as football, rugby, hockey, professional wrestling and boxing.

Is there an instinct for violence in all of us? "Well, not in me of course. It's in those other people. They started it.. I'm willing to fight back against an attacker, to go to war if necessary, but..."

It's impressive to see how quickly military training can bring out the instinct for violence in new recruits. In only a few short weeks, young men and women who have never committed a strongly violent act can be taught to kill and destroy people and property.

People who have studied human violence verify that this instinct is in all of us. It's like this:

Violence is the baseline strategy for most encounters between, and indeed within, species.

(The Nature of Violence, Orion magazine, Jan/Feb 2006)

This is a line in an award-winning essay by Dr. Jeffrey A. Lockwood of the University of Wyoming. He attributed the statement to his mentor, Dr. Jeff LaFage of Louisiana State University, who ironically died in an act of violence, shot in an attempted mugging.

Both these men were entomologists who studied insects and other species. Another scientist, a psychologist and recognized authority on human violence, Steven Pinker, supports the idea that we have an instinct for violence:

> *There are many reasons to believe that violence in humans is not literally a sickness or poisoning but part of our design.*
> *(The Language Instinct)*

Steven Pinker presents an extensive study of human violence in his book, *The Angels of Our Better Nature*. He describes the extreme nature of violence in human history, such as ritual killings, torture, wars and public abuse of victims. Of this violence, he says:

> *Violence is found throughout the history and prehistory of our species, and shows no sign of having been invented in one place and spread to others.*

Despite the long history of this instinct, Professor Pinker documents that although human violence is still all too easy to find in the modern world, it has declined significantly over the ages.

Why did violence decline? What could possibly overcome the force of our instinct for violence? In a word: culture. Over the past few centuries, we've been developing a culture of peace and empathy, and this has curtailed our instinct for violence.

Dr. Pinker describes a number of cultural developments that have reduced violence. Some of these are: the rise of widely-trusted strong central authorities replacing feudal warlords, the widespread use of money and its ability to facilitate cooperative trade, and the development of a culture of self control.

The decline of violence is a strong example of how a well-developed culture can modify and redirect an instinct, even a destructive one. Through our typical human process of trial and error, our species has made itself a more peaceful world. Let's hope this process can continue!

Order

Yes, we have an instinct for order. This instinct motivates us to seek order, to like it and to understand it. But our order instinct doesn't decide for us what sort of order we want. It doesn't care whether we have straight lines or neat rows or clean shoes. That's *our* job, the job of developing the culture to satisfy our instinct for order.

In response to this instinct, people have done an extensive job of creating order. It shows up in the way we do things: We stand in lines. We carefully drive our cars between marks painted on the roads. We observe a first-come-first-serve order at restaurants and at four-way stops. We eat our desert last.

Our instinct for order shows up in the way we design things: We place our auditorium seats in rows. We use rectangular sheets of paper. We prefer straight lines and smooth curves in our architecture. We like things to be symmetrical. We lay out our cities and farm fields in neat rectangles.

Our instinct for order shows up in the way we talk. We tend to take turns speaking. We put our words in a traditional order. Words that come in a different order puzzle us, as when Star Wars character Yoda says something like, " When nine hundred years old you reach, look as good you will not."

Our instinct for order shows up in the our rules, regulations and laws. We have traffic lights, speed limits, hunting quotas, zoning laws and Roberts Rules of Order.

Our instinct for order is so strong that we often invent order just for the sake of order. We call this making rituals, and all known societies do it. For us, this includes things like birthday parties, weddings, funerals, ribbon-cuttings and religious ceremonies.

Our instinct for order is strong enough that we can be very upset when our sense of order is violated. A stranger walks across our lawn. A car fails to wait at a four-way stop. Someone cuts in line. A referee makes a bad call against our home team. Someone violates our religious beliefs. Someone burns our flag. Protesters interrupt a funeral burial. We instinctively want our order!

Patterns/Causality

Closely related to our instinct for order (and possibly a part of that instinct) is our instinct for finding patterns and causes. Here's an example: You're watching television. Suddenly the set goes black. What do you do? You immediately start looking for patterns. What happened at about the time the set went dark? Did someone trip over a power cord? Did the lights in the house also go black? Has this happened before? We want to know what caused the problem.

We look for patterns constantly and instinctively. We ask: What's holding up traffic—and which lane will be fastest? What makes Aunt Sadie sad when I mention Uncle Clarence? Which college major will best prepare me for a career?

Animals learn by association. A dog learns to associate getting praise when it responds properly to a command to "Sit!" We humans can do that, too. For example, a child may associate getting a treat with a visit to Grandma's house. But going beyond that association, the human child, by instinct, will look for a pattern: Did I do something cute that caused Grandma to give me the treat? Is there a reason she gave it to me? Does she want me to do something? What's the pattern? What's the reason?

Our instinct to search for patterns and causality is responsible for our greatest human accomplishments. It's the force behind science, engineering, art and many other great deeds.

Reciprocity

We instinctively understand reciprocity. Very young children recognize trading, giving something and getting something in return. As adults, we readily engage in transactions. We instinctively feel obligated to respond to a gift or favor by saying "Thank you" or by giving something back. An unexpected holiday gift can generate an apology, "I'm sorry that I have nothing for you."

Reciprocity is instinctively understood in every known human society. It's the basis of business, where bartering or buying things balances our needs.

But there's a dark side to reciprocity. That instinct is behind the ancient philosophy of "an eye for an eye, a tooth for a tooth," which means a person committing an offense should suffer the same offense or an equivalent penalty in return. It's also the instinct behind revenge, when the reciprocity instinct (along with the anger instinct) generates a feeling of the need to strike back against an offender. And it's involved in our sense of justice, making us feel that an offender should be punished.

Conflict

Want to see our conflict instinct in action? Turn on your TV. Go to a movie. Read a book. What you'll see is a whole lot of conflict.

Conflict is at the heart of the most popular TV shows: the good guys versus the bad guys, or the boys versus the girls. Conflict gets us to the movies to see monsters fighting and love triangles setting old friends against each other. Conflict is in books, plays, even ballets. The classic contest between Prince Siegfried and the evil sorcerer at Swan Lake is typical.

And how about sports? We pay money to watch the home team confront the visitors. We even drive our kids to soccer practice to teach them how to outdo the other team. We value competition.

If there's not conflict, we create it. We transform activities that don't have any inherent need for conflict into contests. We turn band concerts into band contests, academic exercises into quiz programs, painting exhibitions into artist competitions.

Everyone understands conflict. At a very early age, little kids confront each other without any coaching. Their arguments over toys, play spaces and food treats are previews of the disputes between adults later in life. We're often confronted by debates, arguments, contests and fights. It's conflict. It's in every known human society. It's an instinct.

Language

Would you be surprised to know that you can learn a language instinctively? No, all those classes in Spanish and French weren't wasted. But you really didn't need classes to become fluent in your first language (It was probably English, since you're reading this). It's very likely that you learned English quickly, in less than two years, thanks to your language instinct.

Yes, you were born with a language instinct, one that motivated you to start looking for language as soon as you were able. As a young toddler, you started babbling in meaningless syllables, exercising your newborn ability to make vocal sounds. You heard people around you babbling back, and you tried imitating the sounds they made.

Each of us is born with an instinct for language. We start life searching for language and we learn our first language very quickly, thanks to our instinct for grammar. Whether we are learning English, Spanish, Swahili or !Kung, we already understand that our language, when we find it, will have a certain grammar, a certain basic structure that's common in all naturally acquired human languages.

We instinctively know that there's singular and plural, present, past and future tense, and other basic rules of grammar. Very young English speakers may mess up their words a bit, saying "My teacher *holded* the baby rabbit" instead of "My teacher *held* the baby rabbit," but their grammar instinct gets the tense right, even before they get the exact words right.

Our language instinct is eloquently described by psychologist Steven Pinker in his aptly-named book, *The Language Instinct*. Among his comments, he says, "...language is the product of a well-expressed biological instinct..." and "There is a universal grammar that governs all naturally acquired human languages."

Professor Pinker also describes in great detail how we learn language, telling why it's so easy to learn our first language and so difficult to learn a second language. He explains that the newborn brain is loaded with neurons that make the learning easy, but that the brain loses those neurons later, so that it's much harder to learn language after the age of six.

Morality

Everyone has a sense of what's moral. Throughout our lives we hear about it from our parents, from our governments and from our religious leaders. And we end up with a variety of ideas about exactly what is moral. But no matter what set of morals we have, we all agree on some things; for example: Lying, cheating, stealing and killing are bad things.

It seems that we all have a basic instinct for morality, a need to behave according to some pattern. And moral patterns can be seen in all human societies. This is evidence that the need for morality is an instinct.

But exactly what does our moral instinct tell us? Are we humans kind and altruistic beings? Or are we mean and selfish? The answer is: Yes, we have both good and bad behavior within us.

For the positive side, let's ask Robert Wright, who wrote a book called *The Moral Animal*. Mr. Wright says, "Friendship, affection, trust—these are things that...hold human societies together." And another author, Matt Ridley, says, "Our minds have been built by selfish genes, but they have been built to be social, trustworthy and cooperative" (*The Origins of Virtue*).

Both authors bring up the model of *reciprocal altruism*, an instinctive behavior also nicknamed "Tit for Tat." It's basically a variation of The Golden Rule that means "Do unto others as they have done to you." It means that at first encounter we treat the other person cooperatively. Thereafter, we do whatever the other one did in that first encounter.

Reciprocal altruism means that one good turn deserves another, and so good behavior is perpetuated. "...this instinctive cooperativeness is the very hallmark of humanity and what sets us apart from other animals," says Matt Ridley.

But there's a negative side to this approach, according to Robert Wright. He points out that

> *"with reciprocal altruism the goal is that the organism be left under the impression that we've helped; the impression alone is enough to bring reciprocation...hence the general tendency of people to burnish their moral reputations; reputation is the object of the game... And hence hypocrisy."*

Instincts are nearly always activated through culture. And culture can change the way the instinctive morality is expressed. For example, lying isn't always bad. It isn't bad to lie if you're captured by an enemy. Cheating isn't bad if you're an undercover detective. Stealing isn't bad if you're repossessing a car. Killing isn't bad if you're killing an animal needed for food or someone threatening your own life.

Our different cultures have given us strikingly different codes of conduct, all based on the same basic instinct. We're still learning about the content of this basic instinct and we're trying to understand how it's expressed in our culture. We still have a lot to learn about our instinctive morality.

Spirituality

There's good evidence that spirituality is an instinct. Human societies all over the world have been chasing spirits for as long as we have records. People have been worshipping supernatural beings and attributing special qualities to objects and animals for thousands of years.

More than two thousand years ago the ancient Greeks invented a world of gods and goddesses living on Mount Olympus. Even earlier than that, the ancient Egyptians worshipped a variety of gods, pharaohs, and even bulls and cats.

In their quest for spirits, people have created many myths of supernatural beings. To the Boshongo people of the Congo, the creator of the universe was the god Bumba, who vomited up the sun, the moon, the stars, the animals and the people. Another god, Lord Vishnu, was the ancient Chinese people's creator. After having slept for 18,000 years inside an egg, he broke out of it and the contents of the egg formed the earth and the sky.

These ideas may seem silly by our standards, but these ancient people truly believed in their spirits. For example, in very old Mexico, the Aztecs saw the sun as a spirit named Huitzilopochtli (Tonatiuh for short). Their belief in this sun god was so strong that they conducted horrible human sacrifices to appease that imagined spirit to make sure the sun would rise again every day.

In ancient Egypt and China people believed the human body could be inhabited by spirits, and disease was a indication of an angry spirit.

As our knowledge of science advanced, our spiritual beliefs became more and more practical. Still, even today we continue to have exorcisms and séances and spiritual readings, all attempting to contact spirits.

This fascination with spirits in all these diverse and disconnected human societies shows a motivation strong enough to be an instinct. While spirituality hasn't been established as an instinct yet scientifically (Could some of these spirits be real?), there's evidence enough that we're including spirituality here in this list as a probable instinct.

Acquisition/Possession

Do we have an instinct for acquisition? Do we have an innate need to possess things? Probably.

Wherever people congregate you'll find shops, stores and shopping malls, eager to cater to our desire to acquire things. Our closets are never big enough to hold all the "stuff" that we want to possess. Whatever we have, we seem to always feel the need to want more.

When archeologists dig up the remains of old civilizations they usually find evidence of tools, art objects, weapons and other items that were the "stuff" of earlier people's closets. Back when people were living in caves, their "stuff" even included jewelry, beads that some scientists believe were the objects of very early trade; that is, very early acquisition.

Male and Female Instincts

Do the males and females among us have different instincts? The evidence is very strong.

Until recently it was fashionable to assert that women and men are exactly equal. Perhaps it's partly the result of political movements like women's suffrage and women's liberation. It became popular to say that there were no differences between the sexes and, therefore, no reason to discriminate between them. But equality doesn't mean that women and men are the same.

As recently as 1990, a groundbreaking book called *You Just Don't Understand* announced specific differences between the sexes. This book was the result of surprising research by Deborah Tannen, a linguist who discovered that when women and men talk, they reveal typical differences in their thinking. While the point of this best-selling book was to show that these differences produce communication misunderstandings between the sexes, it helped launch further study of those differences.

Written in crisp, academic style, Tannen's book was followed by other more general-audience books, some by Tannen and another hugely popular book by John Gray, *Men are from Mars, Women are from Venus*. Gray's book expanded the subject of gender differences to all aspects of men's and women's social styles.

But these books didn't identify these differences between the sexes as instincts. That, however, is what we're doing here, as a probable instinct that's being confirmed on a regular basis by all the study that's now going on. For example, scientists are discovering that there are real differences in the brains of men and women. Women's brains have a wider connection between the two halves, and they have a larger communication center. Other typical differences by sex have been found in the brain regions involved in memory, emotion, vision, hearing and navigation.

Research is showing that men tend to be more independent than women, they tend to be more logical in their decisions, and they are more aggressive. Women tend to share their problems, are more emotional in their decisions, and avoid conflict.

Social instincts

We're the ultimate social creatures. We sing, "People who need people." We recite, "No man is an island." We say, "All of us are better than one of us."

We sing about it, talk about it, and gather together to help each other as we've done since Day One. We live in societies, we build cities, we form associations, we take partners.

We're not the only social creature, of course. Ants and bees live in intricate social colonies that resemble our own cities. Each ant has its own role in the anthill, and each bee grows up equipped for its own special function in the hive. Beavers get together to build their dams. Wolves hunt in packs. They do this by instinct.

But we humans are equipped to go far beyond our insect and animal neighbors. We're far more adaptable. We use our big brains to devise social groups that can adapt to a variety of situations. We can easily change the purposes of our social groups and change the groups' members, sending out some of us to build buildings, others to attend parent-teacher meetings, others to serve in army rifle squads, and others to be golfing foursomes. In short, our social activities involve not just a social instinct, but also huge measures of culture.   69

Our social instincts are so strong that they show up in many different forms. Here are some key social instincts:

Social acceptance (a social instinct) - We instinctively seek acceptance from other people. We groom ourselves and behave in ways that have no direct benefit to ourselves, but which we hope will influence others to accept us. We smile, we speak in friendly tones, we give presents, we do favors, we dress in clothing of the current fashion, we bathe and brush our teeth in hopes that others will like us.

If other people accept us into a club or activity that we seek, we're happy. If we receive an award that indicates that other people recognize our importance, we're elated. We consider it a great punishment to be shunned; that is, to be expelled from a group.

Gregariousness (a social instinct) - We cling together. We seek out the company of other people. This seems to be an instinctive characteristic that we all have.

Whenever there's a crowd of people, often more people will come over and join the group. When we celebrate something, like birthdays, graduations, promotions and the like, we usually do it in groups, the more the merrier. We form associations for everything from quilting to stamp collecting.

All over the world, people are coming together in settlements, towns and cities. This is a long-established trend to live close to lots of other people. In 1950, less than 30% of the world population lived in cities. In 2008 more than half of the people in the world were living in cities. By 2030 the urban population will have swelled to 60%. It will go up to 70% of us living in cities by 2050, according to United Nations figures.

Recognition of one's own kind (a social instinct) - To be so gregarious, it's handy to be able to recognize one's own kind. And we can do that, just like other living creatures. Geese fly in gaggles, fish swim in schools, cows hang out in herds. They have an instinctive ability to recognize others of their own kind.

We also have that instinct. Without any thought, we've always been able to recognize another human being. This may result in a friendly encounter or a confrontation, but when we see a creature that's like us, we recognize it.

Of course, culture is involved in the way this instinct plays out in our real lives. History is full of accounts of people becoming convinced that certain other humans, ones of a recognizably different race, religion or nationality, are less than human. This negatively-focused culture has produced some of the most shameful events of our history.

Some of the our most noble history has come from creating a positive culture that says that those other humans are indeed people and are acceptable to us.

In either of these cases, positive or negative, our instinct to recognize our own kind is active. But our culture can trigger another instinct, the friend-or-foe instinct. You'll read about this instinct next.

Friend and foe (a social instinct) - This idea is well expressed in a quote that has been attributed to many public figures: "He's a so-and-so, but he's OUR so-and-so" (You can substitute your favorite derogatory term for "so-and-so"). To translate this, it means that the person in question is a friend, and regardless of his character, he's on OUR team.

We readily classify others as friends or foes. We do this in happy games. We do it in serious political contests. We do it in deadly wars. We've been doing it throughout human history.

There's always some way we distinguish between our friends and our foes. It may be something as simple as two lists of names indicating who is who. It may be some physical characteristic like length of hair or style of clothing. It may be some behavior, such as speaking a certain language or performing certain rituals.

We look for these distinguishing characteristics and once we find them, we treat friends and foes in vastly different ways. We instinctively support and protect those we classify as friends. We instinctively oppose and attack those we classify as foes. We do this whether it's a friendly game or a nasty feud.

You can feel this friend/foe instinct inside you if you happen to witness a ball game between two teams you're not familiar with. Without much effort you may feel yourself picking a favorite team and rooting for it. You've picked a "friend" and a "foe." It's instinctive.

Advertisers often use the friend/foe instinct to sell you things. A television commercial will sometimes show two people arguing over the product the advertiser wants you to buy. One person is a smart, charismatic user of the product, the other person is a more crude and less intelligent person who doesn't use the product. The advertiser knows that you may instinctively pick a side of the argument and will probably identify with the smart person. That would make you more favorable to using the product, to the delight of the advertiser.

Protection of children (a social instinct) - "Of course we protect our children!" It's hard to imagine anyone who would dispute this statement, so strongly do we feel this instinct. The face of a child can elicit feelings strong enough to motivate us to smile and make cooing sounds. It's hard to resist making baby talk when you're talking to a baby.

But we can be manipulated by persons who use our protective instincts to induce us to support certain causes. "It's for the kids" is a slogan that regularly raises funds for a children's hospital. To get us to support their proposals, politicians often emphasize any benefits to children that may exists in their ideas.

Search for a leader (a social instinct) - "Who's in charge here?" That's a question we often ask when we find ourselves in an unfamiliar situation. We seem to have an instinctive urge to seek a leader.

The founding fathers of the United States believed the country should have a president. The people of Great Britain believe they should continue to have a queen. Committees have chairpersons. Sports teams have coaches. Businesses have CEO's. Indian tribes have chiefs. It seems that wherever groups of people get together, we instinctively look for a leader.

This is the instinct that has allowed people to be led by kings, dictators, religious despots and politicians. We assume that in nearly every situation, somebody must be in charge, so we accept leadership that we might question otherwise.

And sometimes, when we've found the great leaders we seek, we've accomplished great things.

Aesthetics

Even if we didn't do well in art class, each of us has an instinct for things that are pretty. Some of us react to art in a gallery or to music in a concert. Some of us like the feel of fine furniture or the aroma of bread baking. For some of us, it takes the new car models to bring out our sense of what looks good. All of us respond to the way things look, feel, smell, sound and taste.

There are many aspects to our aesthetic instincts. Here are some of them:

Facial recognition (an aesthetic instinct) - We're well-equipped to recognize faces. Our school yearbooks are full of them. Each face is smiling back at us, knowing that we'll recognize the precise placement of the eyes, nose and mouth, and the shape of the face and, in an instant, we'll know, "That's George. That's Nancy." It's an instinct.

It's good that we can recognize faces so well. Our survival depends on it. Our ancestors had to quickly recognize friend or foe. Today we still need to identify the faces around us to succeed in our business and our social lives.

And in selecting our mate, facial recognition is a key factor, since we seek an attractive face. In women, attractiveness means large, widely-spaced eyes, high cheek bones, a small chin and full lips. In men, it means an oval or rectangular face, heavy brow ridges, deep-set eyes and a prominent chin.

These aren't just the latest fashion trend. They are facial features identified as being attractive in scientific studies done among both men and women in many different cultures. Psychologist Nancy Etcoff reports in her book *Survival of the Prettiest* that "Cross-cultural studies have been done with people in Australia, England, China, India, Japan, Korea, Scotland and the United States." She also lists studies done in Brazil, Russia, and among Hiwi and Ache Indians. Obviously, our perception of facial beauty is instinctive.

As in our other instincts, facial recognition is centered in the brain. A large portion of our brain is involved in recognizing faces. An area called the fusiform gyrus is believed to be the center of this brain activity, and it's linked to an entire network of areas of the cerebral cortex.

Music (an aesthetic instinct) - Everywhere people are, there's music in some form. When drums beat or hands clap, when instruments start playing or voices start singing, people join in by dancing, clapping, singing or tapping their feet. Small children respond to music so strongly that school teachers often use music as a teaching tool.

Rhythm is an instinctive part of music. When the beat begins, it's hard for us to resist the instinctive urge to sway to the beat. *Melody* is another instinctive aspect of music, and we can easily follow a series of notes. *Harmony* in music is also instinctive, and, without any music lessons, we recognize when groups of notes sounded together are pleasing or not.

But do we all instinctively like the same kind of music? Not at all! We all respond to rhythm, melody and rhythm by instinct. But our culture gives us different preferences. Some of us have learned to favor music that's classical, some like rock, others choose country or jazz or even bagpipe music or rap. It's a matter of culture. We learn to like the music we like.

How strong is our musical instinct? On May 29, 1913 at the Théâtre des Champs-Élysées in Paris, Igor Stravinsky introduced his new musical composition, *Rite of Spring*. This was very different from the traditional graceful and elegant ballet music that 1913 audiences expected. Instead, this new music was full of jagged rhythms and repeated chords with dissonant notes clashing together. As the music started, the audience began to react instinctively to the unfamiliar sounds. Soon they became so upset that they began booing, arguing and throwing punches. Eventually, the police had to be summoned to break up the riots. But one year later, after audiences had become accustomed to hearing this sort of music, the piece was being performed to great acclaim.

The music instinct was strong enough to motivate those sedate, elegant people to riot and fight over the unfamiliar and unpleasant sounds. But over time, culture intervened as the people became familiar with the new music and learned to like it.

Our musical instincts give us evidence that the strength of certain instincts may be different in different people. Some individuals respond strongly to rhythm and other musical elements, while other individuals have difficulty with music. Being "tone deaf" appears to be a natural condition, but we all do have the musical instinct—just like those people in Paris!

Rhyme (an aesthetic instinct) - Rhyme is an instinct we all know. You seem to find it wherever you go. In music, in poems, we follow its flow. It's instinctive, it grabs us, and it won't let go. If we saw it we'd know it, don't you think so?

Summary note

At last you've reached the end of this long but incomplete list of our instincts. It's a long list because it includes some instincts that are well documented, along with others that are apparent but not yet fully studied. It's incomplete because there certainly must be other instincts yet to be recognized and described.

Many scientists and academics are busy making discoveries that can extend this list. They're making slow progress, even though the answers to our curiosity are in plain sight, waiting to be recognized. They're right here inside us motivating every action we take, all day, every day. And every day, as we see them better, we learn more and more about our human instincts, this wonderful force within us.

We're animals. We're born like every other mammal and we live our whole lives around disguised animal thoughts.

—Barbara Kingsolver, Animal Dreams

Chapter 12
The Author's Comments

I had to write this book. Someone had to. We all need to know the answer to the question, "What are we really like?"

People have been struggling for ages to figure this out. It's a question that has challenged philosophers, psychologists, politicians, scientists—just about everybody. And the answers still aren't all here.

The trouble is, we've been trying to look at ourselves. And that's really hard. It's like trying to figure out what you look like if you don't have any mirrors. You may be walking around with your hair sticking up or with dirt on your face. You won't know about it. You can't see it.

That's the kind of thing we humans have been doing since Day One. We've been trying to figure ourselves out. We've needed to know about ourselves because we live with other people all the time. We work with people to accomplish things. We depend on people. We need people to survive.

And working together, we've made progress. But we're still not there. We still make big mistakes. We still have problems dealing with each other. And we still have big questions about what makes us tick.

That's why I had to write this book, to do what I can to help answer the important questions about ourselves. Like everybody else, I've been working on understanding people for all my life. That's more than seven decades so far. In that time I've earned a lot of titles, including student of psychology, sociology and philosophy, businessman, pilot, soldier, author, photographer, artist, journalist and, most importantly: parent, neighbor, friend, and book reader. I've studied and observed people, and I've learned a lot about us. And in all that study, I've never seen the answers as you're reading them in this book. I've also never found any source that had better answers, none that could show how the answers in this book are wrong. And, believe me, I've been looking.

So here's my book. Here are my answers. What you're reading here may seem a little odd at first. That's natural. In our study of ourselves, we've been very reluctant to look at our genetic makeup; that is, we've been slow to recognize what's built into us by nature.

We don't like to think of ourselves as animals. We want to be superior. We want to be divine. We don't want to think of ourselves as being driven by instincts. "No, that's the way animals are," we think. "Animals do just what their instincts tell them, but not us. We're superior. We have language. We use tools and have opposable thumbs and we live at the top of the food chain."

So we pretend to be something other than what we really are. We hide our animal bodies under clothing. We surround ourselves with enclosures that separate us from the natural world. We build tools that give us superior capabilities, like cars that make us go faster than any animal, computers that give us expanded intelligence and devices that go up in the air. "We can fly," we say. But we really can't. We can build machines that fly and ride in them, but we have no natural ability to fly—or to do any other similarly wonderful thing without help.

If we had that magic mirror to look at ourselves, we'd see that we have constant reminders of our physical nature. Every few hours we must pick up plant and animal material (we call it "food"), put it in our mouths and chew and swallow it. We ingest water, often with substances added so we can have tea, milk, cappuccino or Coca Cola. Like other animals, eventually we must eliminate the remains of that digested plant and animal material and water. If we get hot, all over our bodies our skin secretes a liquid to evaporate and keep us cool. If we get too cold, our skin lifts our thousands of hair follicles and forms "goose bumps" and our muscles begin to shiver involuntarily to generate heat. And as often as every few seconds we must take in air containing oxygen or, within minutes, we will perish.

We are indeed animals. We share the exact same kind of DNA as all other animals—and even all plants. Our skeletons are modified versions of the skeletons of other animals, with a bone elongated here, another bone reshaped there.

Like animals, we do have instincts. We inherited them from our ancestors along with our bodies and our brains and they are of basic importance to understanding our true nature.

But you don't have to believe that people are animals to understand about our instincts. You don't have to have any particular viewpoint, no particular philosophy, religion or scientific understanding. All you have to do is look around you. You can see it in how we people conduct ourselves. And you can feel your instincts inside you.

But if we're driven by instincts in everything we do, where's the nobility of the human race? Where's the capacity to do wonderful things, to make our lives and the world better?

Our nobility is in our culture! Our greatness is in what we do in response to our instinctive motivations, and that's our culture.

To date, psychologists, sociologists and other scientists have made remarkable progress in understanding our true nature. They've defined aspects like drives, emotions, personalities, and also some of the instincts we've talked about right here. And they have some excellent new tools to investigate ourselves, things like functional MRI, which allows us to look inside a brain while a person is doing things and see that brain in action.

Despite this progress, we still find many people's behavior to be puzzling. But it's really more simple than that.

Every aspect of human nature has to be either: 1) Something we're born with that's built into our brains and our bodies, or 2) Something we've devised and learned. That is, it's all either 1) instinct, or 2) culture.

This book follows that simple approach to understanding ourselves. I don't want to discard any of our current progress. I want to build on it. I want to keep the knowledge of instincts that's well established. But I want to encourage further study to discover and define as much of our instinctive heritage as possible.

Once we accept the role of instincts in our lives and understand these instincts more fully, we'll be better able to devise ways to satisfy them. We'll be better able to achieve the selfish happiness that we all instinctively crave. We'll be able to deal with our instinct for conflict without war. We'll be able to satisfy our instinct for social acceptance without conquest. We'll be able to respond to our instinct for anger without a fight. We'll be able to understand each other without argument.

That's why I wrote this book. I want us to recognize that we have instincts and I want us to continue the ages-old quest of learning about them. I want us to pick up that magic mirror that lets us see ourselves as we really are, not as we pretend to be. And I want us to do a better and better job of devising ways to satisfy our instincts to produce the best results for all of us.

Our instincts are the force within us that will keep setting us in motion. But it's our culture—the things we do to satisfy our instincts—that will ultimately make us the noble creatures we seek to be.

—Paul Bergen Abbott

Index of instincts in the lists

A Book List

These are a few of the books that provided inspiration and substance for this book. If you would like to know more about human instincts, these will save you lots of searching. They are listed here in the chronological order of their first publication.

The Selfish Gene by Richard Dawkins, 1976 and 1989, Oxford University Press. A groundbreaking book on how characteristics are genetically inherited. An introduction of the concept of the selfish aspect of biological nature.

You Just Don't Understand by Deborah Tannen, 1990, Ballantine Books. This best seller introduced differences between the behavior of women and men, based on how they talk.

Human Universals by Donald E. Brown, 1991, McGraw-Hill. An extensive list of those features of culture, society, language, behavior, and psyche that exist in all known humans.

Men are from Mars Women are from Venus, The Classic Guide to Understanding the Opposite Sex by John Gray, 1992, HarperCollins. A popular book that introduced to many people the idea of different social styles of men and women.

Anatomy of Love by Helen Fisher, 1992, Fawcett Columbine. A natural history of mating, marriage and why we marry.

The Moral Animal, Why We Are the Way We Are by Robert Wright, 1994, Random House. How our biological nature guides the choices we make throughout life.

The Language Instinct, How the Mind Creates Language by Steven Pinker, 1994, William Morrow and Company. Explains how language is wired into our brains as an instinct.

The Origins of Virtue, Human Instincts and the Evolution of Cooperation by Matt Ridley, 1996, Penguin Books. Examines the roots of human trust and virtue resulting from self interested instincts.

The Alphabet versus the Goddess, The Conflict between Word and Image by Leonard Shlain, 1998, Viking Penguin. How cultural inventions like the alphabet, film, computers and advertising have affected the brain.

Survival of the Prettiest, The Science of Beauty by Nancy Etcoff, 2000, Anchor Books. Describes how physical characteristics are perceived as attractive.

The Blank Slate, The Modern Denial of Human Nature by Steven Pinker, 2002, Viking Penguin. Defends the role of genetics against the idea that people are born without innate traits.

Nature via Nurture, Genes, Experience and What Makes us Human by Matt Ridley, 2003, HarperCollins. Describes how human instincts and culture determine what we are.

The Agile Gene, How Nature Turns on Nurture by Matt Ridley, 2003, Harper Collins. How humans are simultaneously free-willed and motivated by instinct and culture.

Why We Love, The Nature and Chemistry of Romantic Love by Helen Fisher, 2004, Henry Holt and Company. Explains the physiological aspects of sexual attraction including the effects of brain chemistry.

The Magic of Reality, How We Know What's Really True by Richard Dawkins, 2011, Transworld Publishers. Answers questions many of us might wonder about: What are things made of? What is the sun? What is magic?

The Better Angels of Our Nature, Why Violence has Declined by Steven Pinker, 2011, Penguin Books. Describes the history of human violence and the trend for it to decline up to the present.

www.ingramcontent.com/pod-product-compliance
Lightning Source LLC
Chambersburg PA
CBHW050555280326
41933CB00011B/1858